UNDEFEATED

UNDEFEATED

The story of Bali bombing survivor
PHIL BRITTEN

**WITH REBECCA BRITTEN
& MALCOLM QUEKETT**

UWA PUBLISHING

First published in 2012
by UWA Publishing
Crawley, Western Australia 6009
www.uwap.uwa.edu.au

UWAP is an imprint of UWA Publishing,
a division of The University of Western Australia

THE UNIVERSITY OF
WESTERN AUSTRALIA
Achieve International Excellence

Printed by Griffin Press
Cover image by Lincoln Baker

National Library of Australia Cataloguing-in-Publication entry
Undefeated: the story of Bali bombing survivor
Phil Britten / Phil Britten, Rebecca Britten, Malcolm Quekett.
ISBN 9781742584560 (pbk.)
Britten, Phil.
Victims of terrorism – Australia – Biography.
Bali Bombings, Kuta, Bali, Indonesia, 2002 – Personal narratives.
Britten, Rebecca; Britten, Phil; Quekett, Malcolm.
363.3250959862

To my mum for giving me life.
To Mira, Tansen and Sai for saving my life.
And to my wife, Rebecca, and our children
for showing me the meaning of life.

CONTENTS

Preface: A moment in time, 1

Introduction, 5

1 A life-changing decision, 9

2 The time of our lives, 17

3 Escape from terror, 27

4 The rescue, 37

5 Mira, Tansen and Sai, 45

6 Surviving Sanglah, 51

7 The evacuation, 59

8 Crucified and mummified, 65

9 A mother's view – hearing the news, 73

10 Living in a nightmare, 79

11 The long road home, 87

12 A mother's view – bedside vigil, 97

13 Dale Edgar – RPH Physiotherapist, 101

CONTENTS

14 Day in day out, 107

15 Lacing the boots back up, 115

16 Back to Bali, 125

17 The first anniversary, 133

18 Opening up, 143

19 Falling in love, 151

20 Bali targeted again, 157

21 Ready to move on, 161

22 Two steps forward, one back, 167

23 Stepping up for peace, 177

24 A wife's perspective – Rebecca Britten, 181

25 A mother's view – looking back, 189

26 My message is simple –
appreciate, embrace and love, 191

In Memoriam, 195

PREFACE

A moment in time

THAT'S ME, BLOODIED AND COMPLETELY BEWILDERED, perched up there on that wall. I was escaping from the Sari Club in Bali, which had just been blown apart by terrorists on October 12, 2002.

That photo was running nationally in an Australian magazine while I was in intensive care in Adelaide, South Australia. The story of the Bali bombing was being told everywhere, on television and radio news, in the daily papers and in every magazine. Someone somehow realised it was me and, partly in shock, showed me the photo.

It was too much. Looking at that photo, the memory of what had happened just a few days earlier, took me right back to that place and I couldn't take it. I passed out.

That was the first time I'd ever seen myself in a magazine. Looking back, I realise how that photo captured an exact moment that defined my life so clearly between "past" and "future". My past is "before Bali" and my future is everything "after Bali".

Before Bali, I was sailing along comfortably in life, heading towards a pretty predictable future of being a tradie and chasing a footy dream. That moment in time, captured in this photo, shows the exact point at which it all changed and I now had to take a new path, one I had to create for myself. The easy road was gone.

Another thing that comes to mind when I see that photo is how on September 11, 2001, I sat, safely in my living room, watching TV with the world as the World Trade Center in New York collapsed, how Americans had been murdered by terrorists while going about their everyday lives.

I remember thinking: "Thank God, I live here in Perth, in Australia, where that type of thing just doesn't happen."

I had no idea that exactly one year, one month and one day later I too would be caught up in a terrorist attack.

For me to tell you where I went to from here, from being stuck on that wall, I need first to explain where I'd come from and the life I'd led until that point, the life I now had to leave behind.

INTRODUCTION

I WAS FLAT ON MY ARSE. I lay there for a split second, pushed up hard against the bar. It was pitch black and there were bits of the wall, pieces of roof and, I started to realise with horror, body parts all over me. It felt as if I'd been hit by a bulldozer.

For an instant, I didn't hear anything, and then there was a ringing in my ears but no other sound. Just silence. I must've been one of the first to come to, because it was quiet for what seemed like ages, but was probably no more than a few seconds. I'd been walking towards the back of the club when the bomb exploded, but something had knocked me right around and now I was disoriented, facing the front.

I pulled myself up off my back, up onto my knees and grabbed my mouth. The pain was intense. I didn't know what had caused it. I just knew my mouth had been smashed in, and when I took my hands away from my face and looked down at them I saw they were covered in blood. I reached up to touch my head and noticed what felt like a dent in my skull, with my hair already warm and sticky with blood.

October 12, 2002 – a night that changed everything for me. It was a long time before I could stop letting it define me and instead grow to accept what happened as just a part of my journey in life.

I've lost count of the number of times people have asked me: "What happened to you?"

I've realised that I don't want what happened to me, my family, and so many other families to be forgotten.

I want people to understand what happened, not only to me but also to my friends, and many others.

I want them to be able to understand the physical and mental impact, and how, in a split second, life could never be the same.

I've noticed that when I talk about my journey and how I've chosen to deal with it, people are able to draw some inspiration, which perhaps they can apply to their own lives. They're often moved to race home and tell their loved ones how much they mean to them. Sometimes, if just for a moment, they change their outlook on life. And at other times, that new outlook may last just that little bit longer.

So a book is the next step.

If I can reach more people by writing a book, if I can inspire more people to be better human beings, to reach more goals, to treasure their loved ones more, then I will have achieved something real and powerful and positive. And maybe that's why I survived.

So here is my story.

1

A life-changing decision

I ENJOYED A REALLY FREE-SPIRITED CHILDHOOD. My earliest memories of growing up revolve around being outdoors in the sun, the surf and hanging out with my friends. I was always pretty active and fit, and I loved playing sport. And it was this boundless energy that probably helped me years later, when I needed it most, when I needed all the strength I could find just to stay alive.

I moved around a lot when I was young, which helped build a freewheeling attitude to life. I was born in Adelaide and named after my dad, Phil Britten Snr, and was still young when we all moved to Donnybrook, in the south-west of Western Australia.

Not long afterwards my mum and dad broke up, and Mum and I moved to Exmouth, in the north of WA, to be with my grandma and pops, where he was stationed with the US Navy. I was about six years old.

I loved Exmouth and still do. Mum ran a deli and café and we lived in a caravan park for a while. No doors or cars were ever locked and you'd stay out for as long as you wanted. It was summer all year round; life was easy and full of fun. We went camping and fishing and I remember it as such a carefree time. I wasn't the most academic person but was really talented at sport, and in a country town, if you're good at sport, you focus on that. And so that's what I did, day and night. I lived to play sport.

I was lucky enough to be good at just about anything I tried: basketball, tennis, surfing. I loved anything that gave me a physical challenge. But it was Australian Rules football that quickly became my biggest passion.

When I was about eight years old, we moved from the caravan park into town, and this was when I first started playing football seriously and never really looked back. We used to play matches against schools from other towns such as Carnarvon and Tom Price. I started to win a lot of fairest and best trophies, and as

I got a little bit older I was asked to play up the grades with older guys. Everyone used to tell me: "You'll make it one day, you're a talented footballer. You've got to make sure you have a go at it."

Around this time, my mum met Wim, and my brother Ash was born. Wim came into my life when I really needed a father figure, and we became a really close family. Mum and Wim eventually decided to move on from Exmouth, and I think the main reason was that they wanted to give me more opportunities than I could get in the country. We moved to the Perth suburb of Greenwood when I was in Year 9 in high school.

At Greenwood High, I went into footy straight away and started with our local club, Northern Districts. I was used to playing against guys much bigger than me in Exmouth and must have made an impression because it wasn't long before the West Perth Football Club, which plays in the WA Football League, the main semi-professional competition in Perth, noticed me. The WAFL is an important stepping-stone towards making it into the big time, the Australian Football League.

West Perth invited me to join their development squad and I felt that I was on my way. From this moment on, top-class football wasn't just a distant dream any more, but a goal I was working towards, and making significant progress. After that year, Northern Districts folded so I went to Warwick Football Club but continued with the West Perth development squad as well. Footy was my life and I just loved it. I was still at school, but I was playing football six days a week and still couldn't get enough. I was invited to try out for the WA State Schoolboys team, which is the best under -18s in the State. I was selected in the first 60, and kept my place when the squad was cut to 40, and then down to 30.

But probably because I was playing so much football, and giving it everything I had, my knees started to play up and I couldn't go any further with the State team. It was a massive blow to my confidence.

I rested my knees and they slowly recovered, and I couldn't wait to get back on the ground. I was determined to go hard again at football. About this time West Perth showed they thought I had a future. Changes to the WAFL residential qualification rules meant that I might end up tied to a different club because of where we lived. But under the rules of the zone changes West Perth could pick two players to keep. One of the two they wanted was me!

A West Perth football manager came to our home and sat down with my mum and me. We signed an agreement that even though the zones were changing, I would commit to play with West Perth. It was a huge moment in my life and I felt really important. I was signed and locked in to play with West Perth. It was like you read about or watch in the movies; it was like a dream coming true.

Before too long I had my first opportunity with West Perth reserves. I was only 15 going on 16 and was about to play against WAFL adults for the first time. I waited for some time on the interchange bench and didn't think I was going to get a run, but then one of the smaller guys in our team was injured.

The coaches looked down the line at who was on the bench and called to me to get out there. They were actually going to give me a go! I ran onto the ground to the half-forward line, where straight away the ball was kicked to me.

I marked it about 50 metres from the goals, bounced the ball and ran on. There was a teammate on the goal line and an opposition player between him and me. I had two options: I could have a go at kicking a goal or handball it to my teammate who could possibly kick it. In a split second, I just decided to go for it. In the first minute of playing WAFL reserves football, I ran on and kicked a goal. All my teammates ran down the field and picked me up to congratulate me: it was such an unbelievable feeling! I ended up kicking three goals that day and felt on top of the world; it was as if nothing could stop me now. If I could kick three goals in my first WAFL reserves game at just 15, surely I could make it to the next level, the West Perth league side, and then the next level, the AFL. The big time.

But the dream was cut short again. And once again it was my knees that let me down. After just a few more reserves games I pulled up sore. The doctor said I had flat feet, which were rolling my legs inwards and putting pressure on my joints. This time it was more serious.

I had to stop football. I was devastated. I was still in school, but football was my whole life and it felt as if I'd just reached the point where I could have made a go of it. I was really disheartened by it all. I didn't want to go on to do my final year at school. I'd never had any thoughts of going to university and so I left school and got a pre-apprenticeship at Carlisle TAFE, doing refrigeration air-conditioning. After a year of study, I got an apprenticeship with Direct Engineering Services.

It was at this time that I also took up martial arts. I'd always wanted to learn karate as I'd loved it in the movies when I was growing up and always wanted to know that if anything ever happened to me I'd be able to look after myself. I actually started just before I stopped playing football because I'd wanted to do something that would give me the edge on the field, something to get me ahead of the rest who were all trying to make it as well. When football stopped, I focused on my martial arts because I could work around my knee injury and it was actually helping me to get better.

I found a school in Woodvale, which did Zen Do Kai karate, a reality-based martial arts that I found unique. I put all my efforts into becoming a black belt.

I also moved out of home and into a house with four other guys in Karrinyup. It was a typical guys' house: chaotic and messy all the time. We were partying non-stop, and I was surfing, skating and living the life of an 18-year-old. I was having a ball.

I thought I'd put football behind me and that was it, I was done. But after two years of not playing and doing martial arts instead, I'd found that my knees had improved. The guys I lived with played for Kingsley Amateur Football Club, just a local suburban club, not in the WAFL, but it was footy again nonetheless. They kept saying: "Come on, Britts, you used to play footy. Come down and have a kick." So one day I thought "What the hell … " and went along to start training.

I started playing in the Colts team for Kingsley but it wasn't long before I was noticed by the coach of the top team and started playing a few games for their league side. Before long, it was as if I'd never stopped. I won the Association Fairest and Best award, which was the top award for that level, and by 2001, at the age of 20, I was captain of the Kingsley Football Club's league side.

At the beginning of the following season, in 2002, the club decided to go to Bali for the end-of-season trip. At the same time, I saw an advertisement for Camp America and decided to apply. Amazingly, my application was accepted and I was really excited, but it meant I'd be away for three months and would miss the end-of-year footy trip. I discussed America with my girlfriend at the time and she said: "Well, if you do that, I can't guarantee that I'll be here when you get back." So I changed my mind and said to her: "OK, I won't do the three months of Camp America but I'm going on the end-of-year footy trip to Bali."

It was a life-changing decision.

2

The time of our lives

After I'd decided to go to Bali as part of the club trip, I started to get pretty excited. I'd been overseas with my family on holidays, but never without them. It was going to be a big trip, all the boys together just out to have fun.

We decided to start fundraising to help with the costs. People started throwing ideas around and we had some dress-up parties and raffles, but the most memorable part of fundraising was probably the fines system we used. It didn't really raise much money, but we got a lot of laughs out of it and it helped us bond as a group.

We got hold of bottle tops and everyone engraved their football jumper number inside their top. The rule was that you had to have it with you all the time and if someone who was going on the Bali trip asked to see your bottle top and you didn't have it with you, it was an immediate $10 fine. If you lost the top, it was a $50 fine.

The boys started really getting into it and were turning up all over the place at any time just to see if they could catch someone out. Guys were turning up at houses at 3am, waking up whoever lived there by knocking frantically on the door. The boys would answer the door in their boxers or jocks only to find a group from the footy club standing there saying: "Where's your bottle top?"

I put a hole in mine and kept it on my keys, so I almost always had it. It was a really good idea and people started to figure it out and did the same thing. Luckily, I didn't get caught out very often but we all ended up raising a couple of hundred dollars and having a few laughs along the way.

We were having the time of our lives and it felt like the year of our lives. I was turning 22, was captain of the Kingsley Football Club and had won two association best and fairest awards, which meant I'd been recognised as the best player of all the teams in my grade.

I'd also been redrafted by West Perth and was back on track for my dream of playing AFL. It was serious for me now, a future in AFL was close and really possible as I was in my best shape ever. But first I had to see the season out with Kingsley.

Both Kingsley's league and reserves teams made it to the 2002 grand final. The league side that I captained was beaten, but the reserves won. We all shared in the excitement. Just being in the grand final was a great feeling, but to have one of our teams win was awesome.

We all took time off after the grand finals for the 'Mad Monday' party. We then went out celebrating almost every night that week and the guys who had won the grand final wore their medals with pride. It was a big party time for all of us, and pretty soon we were ready to take off on our Bali trip.

The day before I left for Bali, coach Darren Harris from West Perth Football Club gave me a call to double check when I was coming down to start training for the 2003 season. I told him I'd be there as soon as I was back from Bali. We had a quick chat about the next year and I told him I'd give him a call when I was back in a week. That night I went to bed and found it hard to sleep. I was not only excited about the trip but couldn't stop thinking about starting the season with West Perth. This was it, my chance at making it, and I wasn't going to blow it by doing anything stupid while I was away.

On October 12, 2002, all 20 of us met at the Kingsley Tavern about 7 am. We'd had special tour T-shirts made up, which read 'Kingsley Football Club, Bali Tour 2002' and everyone was wearing them. Kevin Paltridge, father of one of the guys on our team, Corey, had organised two limousines to take us to the airport. We stocked up with beer for the ride and by the time we'd made it to Perth Airport, we'd left behind a couple of shopping bags full of empty cans.

Out the front of the airport, we stopped and posed for a few photos. Everyone was laughing and having a good time already. We couldn't wait to get there! Big Stewie (Anthony Stewart) was a seasoned traveller so he started directing us, telling us to "Go do this, do that, fill out your departure card now". He knew what he was doing so we were happy letting him take the lead. But then, as we were checking in, one of the boys noticed that Big Stewis had left his travel wallet behind at the counter, which had his passport, money and documents. We just took it with us but kept it quiet.

It wasn't until he was at the bar that he realised he'd lost it and he tore back down to the check-in counter in a frenzy to look for it. Soon, he was in a massive panic and we finally gave in and handed it over with a few laughs. So much for being a seasoned traveller!

After our flight took off, the party continued. We were chatting loudly, laughing and having a few beers. We must've been getting pretty rowdy and I remember different groups being warned by the airline staff to quieten down. I remember that about halfway to Bali the pilot's voice came over the intercom saying: "If you guys don't settle down, we'll be turning the plane around and continuing on without your group." How different so many things would be today if he'd carried out his threat.

When we landed in Bali, the feeling was just incredible. It was instant culture shock. The heat and humidity hit us as soon as we stepped off the plane, and it set the tone. I remember breathing in the unique aroma of Bali for the first time and being so excited to have finally arrived. We had a couple of mini-buses waiting at the airport to take us to the Bounty Hotel. There were guys walking around in board shorts, girls in bikinis. To me it was like some kind of tropical paradise, just full of people from all walks of life. We couldn't wait for night to come so we could get out on the town.

When we arrived at the Bounty Hotel, Brad McIlroy and I checked in together to share a room. He was a couple of years younger than me but we'd become pretty close through the footy season. We both quickly changed and headed down to the pool. It was late in the afternoon and there was already a crowd milling around for "Happy Hour", which offered two-for-the-price-of-one drinks at the pool bar.

The music was cranking and I ripped off my singlet and jumped into the pool. We ordered a few cocktails and the party had officially started. Around sunset, we started throwing ideas around about what to do that night.

We'd all agreed before the trip that no matter what happened, we'd all have dinner together. That would free up people during the day and later on at night, but would still see us holidaying together as a team, able to catch up and make sure that the whole group was safe. The first night, it was agreed, we'd all go out for dinner and just see what happened from there. One of the guys mentioned a place called Bagus

Bar, which translates into Good Bar in English. We decided that we'd go there first. Little did we know that the decisions we were making for that night would ensure the other plans we were hatching for the days ahead would never come to be.

I went up to my room to get ready, put on a fresh pair of boardies and a singlet, and realised that I didn't have any thongs. I decided to buy some on the way, because there were heaps of market stalls just outside our hotel. One thing I'd noticed by the pool earlier was that there were lots of North Melbourne AFL football players staying at our hotel. As I walked back down past the pool to leave the hotel I saw a big pair of double-plugger thongs, which obviously belonged to one of them, and said with a grin: "Look Macca, thongs...just begging me to take them!"

I slipped these massive things onto my feet and was on my way. They were a few sizes too big but at least I'd sorted out my footwear for the evening and flip-flopped my way out of there. We rocked up at Bagus and were ushered to the back where there was a long table that could seat all 20 of us. I ordered a steak and a Bintang, the local Bali beer. Towards the end of the dinner, I was chatting with Simon Quayle, who was my coach at Kingsley, about my future in football and my plans to go back to West Perth Football Club when I got home.

I loved playing at Kingsley but I knew that I'd been given another opportunity to go for my dream of playing AFL football, and I just had to take it. Everyone was encouraging me to have a go, which reaffirmed in my mind that I was doing the right thing. I remember feeling so excited about my future that night and wondering what it was going to bring.

At the end of dinner, around 9 pm or so, we started talking about what to do next. Did we just want to leave it at that and head back to crash out, or go on and see the nightlife? I was happy to go with the flow so left it up to the other guys to decide.

Before long, we'd all gathered on the road and then walked around the corner to a well-known local bar – the Sari Club. We'd been told it was where all the Aussies went to party and were pretty keen to check it out.

When we arrived out the front, the place was lit up and the music was loud, but there was still hardly anyone inside. It looked like a small bar from the front, made of bamboo, rattan and thatched grass, but it was mostly open air once you got through the front door.

We still had our beers in our hands and the security guard stopped us, saying something in broken English and Balinese. We understood he was saying: "You can't bring those drinks in here." So we drained them on the spot and put our empties in the bin.

When we got inside, it wasn't long before others started to arrive. More groups of footballers, soccer players, girls, and the club began to fill up. We ordered loads of potent jungle juice cocktails, which are a mix of arrack, vodka and fruit juice, and hit the dance floor. I'm not really a big dancer but a circle formed on the dance floor and everyone was laughing and clapping, encouraging each other to keep the atmosphere going. It was our night, it was going to be a night to remember.

The music was pumping. You could feel the bass thumping in your body. I remember an AC/DC song being played and Corey Paltridge doing his best Angus Young air guitar impersonation. Some typical Aussie anthem songs were played and we were all cheering and singing along. Another song that I clearly remember was by Sophie Ellis-Bextor. It was her latest hit, "Murder on the Dance Floor".

I went over to chat to Laurie Kerr, Kingsley's football manager and a close friend of mine. We started talking again about my football career and how much I was going to miss all these guys if I moved on. I started to get a bit emotional about it all. Laurie encouraged me and told me I was doing the right thing and that all the guys were behind me too. I was ready, I just had to start letting go and grab my dream with both hands when I got home. But for now I was a Kingsley player and I was going to cherish this holiday with my mates.

At that moment, I realised I'd been holding on and really needed to go to the toilet. I told Laurie: "I'll be back in a second, mate," and started to make my way across the dance floor towards the back of the club. The DJ was playing Eminem's "Without Me" and the dance floor was packed, people were stomping heavily along with the beat. I'd just reached the area between the dance floor and the back bar when some people started to look around as if they'd heard something.

I kept walking. Next thing you know "BOOM!" Out of nowhere, this God-almighty flash ripped through the club, and through my body, knocking me out.

3

Escape from terror

I DIDN'T THINK ABOUT WHAT HAD HAPPENED. I WAS just overwhelmed by the pain, and all I could think was: "Fuck, this hurts!" My body was a mix of alcohol, adrenaline, shock and fear, all together at once. As I got to my feet, I noticed the smells: the chemicals from the bomb, which were burning my nose, and the smoke, which was getting thicker and thicker. It was a disgusting odour and I choked on every breath as it burnt my throat. Each breath I took was shorter than the one before because of the pain.

Then I heard someone call out in broken English with a Balinese accent: "Just stay calm, everybody, stay calm, it was just a gas bottle." He was in a panic but trying not to sound it. I thought: "Bullshit! As if a fucking gas bottle has done this." My instincts told me this was something else. Something seriously big.

Then the screaming started. Men and women were screaming, as I'd never heard before. Screaming out that they were hurt. Screaming out in fear. Screaming out because they were dying. I could hear people screaming from out on the street, as well as in the club. It was all around me. It started really softly, a moaning or whimpering, then grew louder and louder. It was piercing. It sounded unnatural, as if it was part of a horror movie, and it was terrifying. Somehow it seemed as if all this terror and mayhem was happening around me but I was detached from it and was looking on, like a zombie.

Gradually I began to get my bearings. Others too were slowly rising, as if from the dead, and, like me, were dazed and trying to work out what had happened. I noticed that everything was pretty much flattened. It was as if someone had hurled a huge bowling ball through the club, knocking down everything in its path. More of the roof started to come down, and then the fires started, and quickly built up intensity.

I started to hear flames crackling, and felt their heat. I heard bottles popping from the heat. Pop, pop, pop. Glass was shattering all over the place. The heat became more and more intense. I looked around and couldn't see a way out.

By now there were flames and debris everywhere, and shadows of people in the distance. Some were crawling around, others were still motionless on their knees. Near me people were lying all over the floor, but I didn't register whether they were dead or alive. It seemed like no one was moving and I felt that I was alone.

I looked out towards the front of the club and I couldn't see anyone, just fire. It was the same to my right. I looked to my left, towards where all the guys had been standing. I couldn't see them. I scanned along the wall on the left towards the back of the club. I could see people moving, trying to jump over the wall. A way out!

I can't remember exactly how I got there. I was sort of walking, stumbling. It wasn't far to the wall but it felt as if it took forever to get there. My thongs had been blown off my feet so I was barefoot, walking through glass and bodies on the dance floor. They were scattered about. Some were on top of each other, some next to each other. Some had no arms, no legs. Some had no heads. And they were burnt.

I don't remember seeing any particular faces and I couldn't differentiate male from female. The smell was the worst. And the sound. The noise of the fire was just incredible. It was raging, it was ferocious, it felt as if it was after me. I got to the wall. I knew instinctively that was the way I had to go. In front of the main wall was a smaller one, like a retaining wall, about knee or maybe waist high. I jumped on top of that and looked at the next wall, which was about 3m high. I knew it would take a big effort to get over it but I had no choice. I just went for it, got my arms up at full stretch and my fingers on top of the wall, which was already starting to feel warm. But I didn't get a good enough grip and fell back, bounced off the lower wall and fell straight back into the fire.

I didn't take in that I'd landed in the flames. I didn't even know that I'd been burnt, I had so much adrenaline coursing through my body. I just got straight back up again, looked up at the wall and thought: "How the hell am I going to do this? This is fucking unbelievable!"

Others were doing the same thing, jumping and falling, jumping and falling. I scrambled up and had another go. I must have jumped a bit higher this time. I could feel my grip was better. I felt that I was actually going to be able to pull myself up, to get out. But as I started to climb, I felt hands all over me, grabbing at me, pulling at me, dragging me down. Those behind me were desperately trying to escape too, and they were using my body as a human ladder. We were all just trying to survive. I lost my grip again and we all fell back, down the retaining wall and into the flames.

I lay there for a moment, completely exhausted, unable to get up. For the moment I didn't feel any pain, I was still in pure survival mode. I knew just one thing. I had to get out or allow myself to die. And I began to feel as if that was how it would end, that I had no chance, that I was done. Then I began to feel the flames searing my skin, burning me up, and somehow I found some strength. I got up on my feet a third time.

Looking up, the task overwhelmed me and I felt like giving up, like I was facing the impossible. Inside my head I heard myself saying: "I can't do this, all my energy's gone. That's it, this is the end." There was a pillar on my left and I leaned on it, resting my head on my arm. All of a sudden, flashbacks started, just like it's said to happen before you die. I had flashbacks of growing up, of Mum, of all my family, of all the things I loved and was going to lose. It felt like time was standing still.

Somehow, those thoughts must have inspired me into action. I found some energy from somewhere deep inside. I looked up at the wall again. I jumped up onto the retaining wall and then launched myself up with everything I had. Then there I was! I'd made it; I was up on top of the higher wall and had a chance to get out! I don't remember pulling myself up, it was like I'd summoned this superhuman energy from somewhere. I just went BANG and was on the wall.

I didn't bother trying to figure out how I'd done it or take the time to consider my effort: I knew I wasn't safe yet, not by a long shot. I moved a small way, just a couple of metres, along the top. Not far off the wall was the neighbouring building. Its roof tiles had been blown off. I took a couple of steps and my foot went though the roof, so I just perched myself for a bit to figure out how to get across it.

Then I started to feel the pain from my back. A terrible burning sensation hit me. I ripped off my singlet but because it had melted to my back, it tore away much of my skin with it. I didn't take in what had happened at the time. I just felt that if I didn't get my singlet off, I was going to burn. I just tore it off and threw it back into the Sari Club, which was now engulfed in fire.

I started to crawl along the roof. There were no tiles, just the structure's skeletal remains. It was hard to see anything. It was still pitch black, except for the light from the flames. I clambered over the roof battens. Behind me there were people falling back into the fire and not coming out. I saw one guy in front of me, slightly to my right. He was going the same way I was but he lost his balance and fell through the roof. I don't know what happened to him from there or whether he even made it. Even though I saw it happen, I didn't really register it. I was just moving and reacting without really thinking.

As I clambered higher up onto the roof next to the Sari Club, the screams from inside the building began to get softer, and then they stopped. I suppose people were no longer able to get out. The only screams I could hear now were coming from out in the street in front of the club.

I made it to the other side of the neighbouring roof and flung my feet over the edge. I was sitting there in a daze, shirt off. I felt burnt, and tired, so tired. And I still felt drunk. The adrenaline rush was slightly wearing off. Down in the alley below people were running back and forth, back and forth. It was pandemonium. I saw flashes of light and realised people were photographing me. I looked down and thought: "Why are they taking photos? Can't they see I'm hurt and need help!" I felt completely alone at that moment and even more confused.

It was a long way down and I had to decide how to get off the roof. I now felt furious, and thought: "I'm sitting on the edge of a burning building, I need to get down and people are taking fucking photos? This is bullshit!" So I just launched myself off the roof and landed in a muddy puddle in the alley.

I rolled a bit. People just stood there and looked at me. I got up and started to run. I ran straight out to the right, towards the main street. When I got there, I looked to my right again and saw where the terrorists had exploded a car bomb. There were people lying around with limbs missing and others running around covered in blood or naked because their clothes had been blown or burnt off. It was a nightmarish scene of absolute carnage and more fire, so I turned in the other direction and started to run as fast as I could, away from it all.

I don't think those poor souls, who were behind me inside the club, those who had pulled at me to try to get out, could have made it. I felt I was the only survivor. I don't remember seeing anyone get out. I'd run about 50 metres up the road when I stopped and it all hit me. It was the first time I'd come out of my zombie mode and started to process what was going on. I thought: "What am I doing, where am I going, what the hell happened?" I turned and started to race back to look for my mates.

And that's when three people I'd never met before grabbed me.

4

The rescue

IT WAS TANSEN AND MIRA STANNARD AND THEIR grandson Sai. I found out later they were expatriates who had been at the opening of a friend's store in Kuta, about 30 m from the Sari Club, and had been lucky to survive the bombings themselves. Their car was one of the few that hadn't caught fire parked out on the street and they were heading the wrong way up a one-way street, trying to find their way through the traffic to get to safety.

I had no idea who they were when they stopped their car after seeing me. I was a shocking sight, like a bloodied monster illuminated by their headlights in the middle of the road. Skin was hanging off my back and arms in 30 cm sheets – blood all over my face and body, no teeth. They knew I needed help or would die. They tried to bundle me into their car as I tried to fight them off. I wasn't thinking straight. I thought that maybe they'd caused all this, that they were sent to pick me up and kidnap me.

They were trying to calm me down and told me over and over that they were going to help me. I was screaming at them, and thinking: "Fuck off!!!" They were trying to take me away and I had to go and find my friends.

They kept yelling at me: "Get in the car, get in the car." Even after they'd bundled me in I was trying to get out, trying to jump out of the car window like a crazed animal. I was covering the back seat in blood and my skin was peeling off. I made it hard for them, but they never gave up and slowly they managed to make it clear to me that they were taking me to get help.

They kept telling me "We're almost there, we're nearly there, it's just around the corner" but the car didn't seem to be moving. There was traffic everywhere and we were jammed in for some time. I just kept screaming in agony and couldn't think rationally about any of it.

Despite the terrible pain, I somehow managed to give them my mum's telephone number. They took me to a small clinic about a 30-minute drive away and when we got there, I somehow pulled myself up and sort of fell out of the car. The clinic lights were off but I ran to the door and started banging until a tiny Balinese lady opened it. She looked at me in shock and horror and took a step back as others from the clinic joined her. They had heard the explosion but didn't know what had happened. I don't think anyone did; it was unimaginable.

Mira and Tansen spoke to them in Bahasa and there was a huge commotion and someone else came running in. There was a room of beds and I sat down on one. I was in agony, delirious with pain, sitting upright and screaming out "Help me, help me" and "What the fuck is going on?"

They stood around me in a group and you could see that they didn't know where to start. I was a mess all over. They got a big bottle of saline solution and cotton wool balls and started gently dabbing saline solution on my body. I was still screaming, telling them it was no help.

Tansen reacted to my screams by grabbing the whole bottle and pouring it all over my head. It was the first time I felt any relief from the burning. For a few seconds it was just beautiful but almost instantaneously I began to burn again and the pain overwhelmed me once more.

That was really all that they could do for me there. They weren't equipped to deal with my level of injuries. They spoke together in Bahasa and I understood that they were going to take me to the main hospital, to Sanglah Hospital, and that I had to get in their ambulance.

I felt relief and thought: "OK, we're going to get in an ambulance, this is going to happen, we're going somewhere I can get help." I got up and walked towards their little shed. They opened the door and my stomach dropped. The ambulance was a beaten-up green van. They got in to start it up and it took a few tries to even get the engine running. I walked over to the side door but couldn't pull it open at first, my skin was still peeling off and everything I touched just tore even more away. I finally got it open and looked inside to see only a thin yoga-style sponge mat on the floor. I asked: "Is this it, am I going in here?" They said: "Yes, in here, you've got to go in here."

I got in and lay down. Immediately my back stuck to the bedding and I knew that when I eventually got up, more of my skin was going to rip off. It was just me and the driver going to the hospital. I kept telling myself to stay alive and held on to the thought that I was only just around the corner from the hospital, from help. I slid around on the floor as the van went over the bumpy roads and around corners. I kept yelling out: "Hurry up! Get me to the hospital!"

The journey seemed to take forever. After about 40 minutes we finally pulled in to the hospital compound. The driver leaned into the back and motioned to me as if to say: "Go, go!" So I got up, yanked the door open, thinking with relief: "Finally, I'm here, I can get help." I imagined walking into a clean place full of medical experts with crisp white linen where I'd be looked after.

I managed to walk the 20 or 30 metres to the doors and then went inside to be confronted by absolute chaos. The soothing image I'd seen in my head was instantly shattered.

There was blood everywhere. It was like a horror movie: burnt bodies on beds, crisp and raw; doctors running around covered in blood; other people who were trying to help. Some of the bomb victims just seemed to have scratches; others were bubbling up, choking and dying. Some were already dead, just lying there, still.

No one saw me at first; I just blended into the scene. I was walking around pleading: "Help me, help me, help me." Eventually someone saw me and tried to grab me, before pausing, trying to figure out how to hold me because of my burns. A guy just finally grabbed me and said: "Here, here, here." He motioned for me to sit on a bed. It was a plastic-covered stretcher and instead of it being sterile and white, as I'd hoped, it was covered in blood. Someone else's blood. I said: "No way, I'm not sitting on that!" But I knew I had no choice.

A doctor tried to wipe off the blood but it just kept coming back and back into a little puddle every time he wiped. I gave up and sat down, in a pool of water and someone else's blood. I kept thinking how weird it was, wanting to wake up from this nightmare. And then, with all my injuries, after everything I'd gone through, the first thing they treated was a gash on my head.

I thought it was a small wound compared to the rest of my body but they started to stitch it. No painkillers, no prep, they just started pulling a needle through my scalp. In agony, I felt it go into the skin. As they pulled the thread through and sewed me together, my head would pull up with it: in and up, in and up.

At that moment, I turned and looked around and out of the corner of my eye in the distance, I finally saw a familiar face. Laurie Kerr! The guy I'd last spoken to at the Sari Club. He'd made it! He was bandaged; and, like me, was not wearing a shirt. He looked pretty beaten up but he was alive!

I couldn't speak because of all the smoke I'd inhaled. I just saw him, and he saw me, and we just sort of shook our heads, made eye contact, and that was it. The next thing I knew, I was being pushed down on the stretcher and wheeled into another room.

There were five or six others in the room and no doctors. Some of them weren't moving and looked as if they were asleep, but I found that hard to believe. Others looked like they'd received some sort of basic treatment like me. I just lay there, and started to drift in and out of consciousness. No one spoke English. It felt as if they'd done all they could and I'd been moved out of the way, left now to whatever fate awaited me.

Questions flooded my mind whenever I was conscious. I thought: "What's going on, where am I, who are these people, why is no one helping me?" I tried to call out with my broken voice: "Help me, help me." I was always brushed aside. People would look over and say "Yes, yes, yes" but not pay me any attention. I looked back over towards those in the other beds who were not moving, and inside I begged them to be asleep or unconscious. This couldn't be the place where I was going to die.

As I lay there, I started to feel inside my mouth with my tongue and hands. My teeth had been shattered. One tooth had been blown into the roof of my mouth and was embedded there. I reached inside and pulled a tooth, or the remains of a tooth, out of my mouth. My mouth was smashed but it seemed the rest of my face was fine. I figured I must have been hit by something round, like a ball, not sharp or I'd have been sliced open. I shuddered at the thought as I remembered the broken bodies scattered in the Sari Club.

I called out to whomever I thought might be able to help, holding up my piece of broken tooth. It's weird what goes through your mind when you're in shock. All I could think about was to save my tooth and the old piece of advice I remembered about putting a tooth in milk. I held it up, calling out "Tooth, tooth", trying to get across that it should go into some milk, motioning like I was dipping it into something, saying: "Do I need to?"

A guy just took it from me and dropped it, throwing it away. I was completely bewildered. I just could not understand what was going on.

5

Mira, Tansen and Sai

AUSTRALIAN EXPATRIATE TANSEN STANNARD AND HIS wife Mira, originally from New Zealand, made their home in Bali in 1997. In October 2002 they were visited by their Australian grandson Sai Frame, aged 23 at the time.

On the night of the bombings, they decided to make what was, for them, a rare trip to Kuta to attend the opening of a friend's surf and clothing store. Mira remembered it was about 25 metres from and diagonally opposite the Sari Club. The trio and a friend were standing outside chatting, looking at the street scene and drinking champagne.

Sai had earlier been mingling with a group of young people at the store opening and they had agreed to go to the Sari Club, but, fortunately, were delayed while they waited for a friend to join them. The first bomb went off a little further away at Paddy's Bar.

> Tansen: "The Paddy's blast was the only sound I heard. Then there was a wave of energy and it flattened us. The next thing I knew I was picking myself up."
>
> Mira: "All the lights went out and there was stuff everywhere."

They had been sprayed with glass, but because they had been knocked down much of the deadly debris flew above them.

> Tansen: "If we had been able to stand up we would have been shredded, there wouldn't be much of us left. But it went above us, that's what protected us."
>
> Mira: "I was blown on top of a friend, and covered in rubble. Tansen and Sai had to find me, not knowing if I was alive or dead."
>
> Sai: "Straight after the blast it was just black. The fire hadn't started yet and there was a deathly sort of ringing silence. We were stumbling

around in the dark and then the fire started to rage and the whole place was alight. There was a lot of dust, it was hard to breathe. It took about 15 seconds before people started screaming and calling out 'Where are you?' to their friends and family."

Tansen: "When we got up it felt like we were moving in slow motion. There were people running away and others coming the other way to help. Sai and I found each other pretty quickly, but we couldn't see Mira at first.

"When we found her and managed to free her, we thought she was really badly injured or dead, but actually she was OK apart from glass cuts. The woman underneath her had glass stuck in her head but was able to walk away. You could see people were stuck in the buildings and burning. There was carnage in the streets."

Mira: "I can remember someone saying 'Take Mira to the car', which we had parked about 100m or so away."

Tansen: "The three of us got ourselves together. The car wasn't really damaged much. We got in but the one-way road system was jammed. We managed to do a U-turn; I don't know how we did it. There was glass everywhere and we started to drive down the footpath.

"As the car lights swept around this guy was standing right in front of us. He was a total wreck. His clothes were shredded and he was obviously badly injured. Sai was in the back and we said: 'Grab this guy!' So Sai jumped out and grabbed him, and pulled him into the car. It was Phil. He was saying: 'My mates, my mates, where are my mates?'"

Sai: "He almost looked like a bat because his skin had come off his arms. He was in pain and I don't know how I got him in the car. He was screaming the whole time 'Where are my friends, where are my friends?' We were trying to keep him calm, and telling him we would find them. We knew we had to get him out of there as soon as possible."

Mira: "He was bleeding from a head wound and had lost his front teeth too."

Sai: "I had to hold Phil back, he wanted to get out of the car. But I didn't want to hold him too hard because he was very fragile. I remember having trouble getting his arms close enough to be able to get him in the car and to sit beside him. He had trouble folding them in."

Tansen: "All the traffic, which was one way, had stopped. But somehow we were helped through because we had this guy in the car, we were one of the first coming out carrying somebody injured. We were heading for a medical centre. We knew they had an ambulance there so we thought we would get him there and they could get him to the hospital.

"When we got to the clinic the place was shut, so we started bashing on the door. The staff woke up and we got Phil in there, but they didn't really know what to do. They didn't know a bomb had gone off and they got a little bowl of saline and started to dab it on him. So I got a whole bag of the saline solution and just poured it all over him.

"When we did that he just went 'Ohhhh', like it was the first bit of relief he had had. Then the medical staff got themselves together and got the ambulance and we got Phil's name and his mother's phone number."

Mira: "After the ambulance had gone I rang Phil's mother and woke her up and said there had been a bomb and Phil had been in it, and he was alive and he was at Sanglah Hospital. She didn't really take it in. We rang a close friend who lived nearby and went there and we watched the news and he gave us some brandy."

Tansen: "We managed to get home and just went and lay down. Our heads were pounding but there was blood all over the seats of the car and when it was light I thought: 'I have to get this blood off the car.' I was washing the blood off the seats and was pretty out of it, and neighbours came and saw me and asked what was happening, and then they took over and nursed us.

Mira: "Tansen lost his hearing from the blast and we all, but especially Sai, suffered flashbacks for a long time. We were all far more traumatised than we realised."

Tansen: "Some days later we rang and spoke to Phil's mum, Jayne, and learnt that they had found him. We heard that he was alive and that started our connection. We were like part of the family then and have been ever since."

Some months later the three were flown to Perth by local media to reunite with Phil. They also attended Phil's wedding to Rebecca and remain the closest of friends.

6

Surviving Sanglah

THE NEXT THING I REMEMBER WAS WAKING UP THE following morning: Sunday October 13, 2002. I looked up, turned my head to the left and could see outside the room through an open door into a corridor. Off to my right was another bed. In it was a Balinese girl, and her family were by her bedside keeping her company.

I felt like I'd been poorly mummified. I started to remember that at some time during the night people had come in and wrapped me very loosely in bandages. It was a pretty rough job though, with gaps between the layers, and some bandages were almost hanging off. People would stop at the open door, look

51

in and take a few steps into the room and look at me. I remember getting really angry with them, thinking: "What the hell are you looking at?" It felt as if we were part of a zoo: people were walking past to gawk at the freak show, and we'd been left without any privacy.

At some point I realised I desperately needed to go to the toilet. I slowly pulled myself up to a sitting position and began to move. Somehow I managed to make it off the bed and leaned on the wall as I moved towards the door to the toilet, fumbling with my shorts. I made it just in time but then the room spun and I collapsed, falling face-first into the toilet. The family of the girl in the next bed got me out and helped me back to bed. I was soaked in my own urine. I was a mess.

It was now nearly 16 hours since the bombs went off. I hadn't been given any pain relief, or at least anything that I remember making a difference. I was in agony, drifting in and out of consciousness. People were still coming into the room and looking at me. I realised then they were looking for their own friends or family. I was so out of it, I didn't wonder whether anyone was looking for me. For all I knew, Laurie and I were the only two who'd survived, and I hadn't seen him since I arrived.

An Australian guy, about my age, came in and asked whether I was someone whose name I don't remember. He squinted at me and asked what my name was. I could only just whisper the words "My name's Phil Britten". It hurt my throat to talk and I realised I was unrecognisable. This guy asked if anyone knew I was there. I didn't remember that I'd given my number to Mira and Tansen so I said "No, no".

I gave him my mum's phone number. He dialled, got her on the phone and said: "I'm here with your son, we're in Bali and he's, ah, hurt." He put me on the line.

She sounded really worried, and asked: "Are you OK, are you OK? What's going on, where are you?" Still struggling to talk, I only just managed to whisper hoarsely: "Yeah, I'm OK, I'm alive, there was an explosion." I still didn't really know what had happened. I went on: "I'm just a little bit burnt but I'm at the hospital and am going to be OK. I'm coming home and I'll see you soon."

I knew that I was much worse than I'd let on, but there was no way I was going to let my mum know that I believed I was going to die. I'd realised what bad shape I was in. My injuries meant no one could recognise me, and I could hardly talk. It was a hard phone call to make and it was even harder to hang up. I just wanted to keep hearing Mum's voice. But I didn't want to upset her any further so I said I had to go and hung up, wondering whether I'd ever speak to her again.

Later that afternoon, another guy walking past the door stuck his head into the room. I looked over at him and he looked into my eyes. It was someone I knew! It was Ben Clohessy! He was one of the boys from our footy team! He sort of looked at me, but then he kept walking. I felt a knot in my stomach. He hadn't recognised me and I couldn't speak or go after him. I could only lie there.

I tried to call after him in a faint whisper "Ben, Ben". He was my link to the world, to my life, and he was leaving. But then, a couple of seconds later, his head popped back into the doorway like he'd had a second thought.

He looked hard into my eyes and said: "Phil! Britts! Is that you?" He came up close and finally realised it was really me. He came over and tried to hug me, but couldn't because of the state I was in. All he could do was just pat the top of my head, saying: "Oh Britts! I found you, man. Shit! Oh thank God!"

"Wait here," he said. "I'm going to get someone to get you out of here, just wait here!" I was wondering what he meant by "out of here". I still didn't really know what was going on. He came back with a stretcher on wheels and some people to help him. They got me on the stretcher and wheeled me through some corridors.

I went through some doors and saw a massive room, about the size of a basketball court. There were doctors and nurses and all sorts of medical people. There were lines of beds. It was where the Australians who had been hurt were being taken before being evacuated. A few of the Kingsley footy boys were there.

They knew people had been looking for me and were so happy to see me. They started to give me advice, saying: "You've got to keep moving. If you lie still, your burns will heal up wrong." I remember trying to sit up, to stretch out the skin on my back and it would break open. I was also opening and closing my hands, bending my knees. It hurt so badly, but I knew I had to do it.

It was so hot. Some of the Kingsley boys had fans and were fanning me down, trying to get some air flowing over my body. Pretty soon it all became a bit of a haze and I think my body was starting to shut down. I was battling to stay alive, to breathe, to focus. I lay down and it felt like I was about to die but I held on. I had to.

Strangely, or maybe just because I was an air-conditioning mechanic, I noticed that there was some work going on. Balinese workers were installing air-conditioning split systems in the room to try to cool it down.

I was told there were some planes coming to get us and take us home to Australia. I was told I'd be on the first RAAF Hercules out of Bali for Darwin. It was meant to be about 10 o'clock that night.

A woman with fiery red hair came over to me. I had no idea who she was. She could see how much pain I was in and asked: "Do you mind if I do some healing on you?" I was just lying there, pretty much totally helpless. "Just do whatever you want," I said. I didn't think anything could make me any worse.

She put her hands over the top of me. I just remember fiery red hair and her hands going over my body but not touching me. It was the first feeling of total relief that I'd had. She was performing reiki. I just felt calm and sort of peaceful.

I closed my eyes and drifted off. Whenever I opened them she was still there. I had a feeling of warmth, a sense that everything was going to be all right. After a bit, I woke and she wasn't there any more. The pain started to come back in waves. I wanted her to come back but I knew she had to go and help others like me, I was just grateful I'd had some relief.

The time I expected to be taken out to the plane came and went. I was still there and the agony of waiting was only just beginning.

Others were going out on the flight ahead of me. I felt abandoned and wanted to know what was happening. I was angry that my place on the plane had been taken; I'd been told I was on my way home. All sorts of crazy thoughts ran through my head, such as perhaps I was so badly injured, it wasn't worth putting me on a plane. Maybe they were taking those instead who had a better chance of surviving. Maybe I really was going to die alone in Bali after all.

7

The evacuation

It felt like there was delay after delay after delay. It seemed to me I was losing the battle; I was being left aside to die. So many thoughts went through my head: "I'm just trying to survive, just trying to get to my family. I don't want to die in Bali." I kept holding on to that. If I was going to die, it would be on my terms with my family.

I was still wrapped up roughly in bandages when we finally arrived at the airport. Bandages around my arms, middle and the lower parts of my legs. I could still move my arms a little and was filthy, still wearing the board shorts I'd had on when I went into the Sari Club.

I recognised military uniforms and felt a sense of relief. I felt safe, that I was being looked after now, and that help was here. With all the urgency and chaos around us, I was tagged "Disaster Male 30". That was exactly how I felt – almost unidentifiable, alone, with no one really knowing who I was, my life hanging by a thread. They put a drip into an arm and a doctor told me they were going to give me some pain relief. I still hadn't had any treatment that had made a difference and I was desperate for it. Everyone was reassuring me: "Mate, you're going to be all right. We're right here, you're going to be on the next plane." I just remember thinking, "Thank God." But the pain was never completely gone, only the most extreme edge was taken off with any medication they gave me.

Then there was movement. "Righto, mate, you're on the plane, here we go," they said. It was an RAAF Hercules and we were being stacked up inside in rows, three high. I was the second one onto the plane and put between two others. The guy above me didn't move. His stretcher sagged down to about 25 cm above my face. His blood was dripping down onto me: drip, drip, drip, onto my stomach and body. I was trapped underneath it, strapped down with nowhere to go.

I could smell something terrible all around me: burnt flesh, burnt hair, burnt clothes. It was so hot and noisy. It sounded as if we were flying inside a hurricane, and as we took off the guy in the stretcher next to me started screaming. "Help me, help me, save me, help me, it hurts," he yelled. It went on for what seemed like about half an hour after take-off and then it just stopped. He was silent. I don't know whether he stopped because he'd been given some pain relief, passed out or just slowly died. But after that time, he never made another sound and I assumed the worst.

The whole time I was so thirsty. My mouth felt so dry. At one stage, a medic came around to see whether I was all right or if I needed anything. "I just need a drink," I said. "Sorry, mate," he said. "I can't give you any water because you're too badly injured. You're going to be going straight in for operations." He went away and came back with a plastic teaspoon of ice. That was all I was allowed. I had about five teaspoons of ice on the flight from Bali to Darwin, one about every half an hour.

I was in and out of consciousness. I'd wake up and the guy above me was still dripping and I'd call out as best I could with my burnt throat, trying to be heard above the noise of the plane: "Help, help, I'm thirsty, help, help me." They would give me a little bit of ice but it was never enough. It was like putting a drop of water in a boiling hot pan and bang, it was gone, just evaporating instantly. No matter how much I had, my mouth was still dry, I was still thirsty, and I was still in constant pain.

Finally we slowly descended into Darwin. It was early morning and the sun was just coming up. I realised that because they'd loaded us on through the back of the plane, and as I was the second person loaded on, I'd be the second last one off. Eventually, I was pulled out of the Hercules onto the airport tarmac and the sun instantly blinded me. I usually wore sunglasses and now the sun was beating down on my face without anywhere for me to turn. One of the medical attendants who pulled me out of the plane was wearing sunglasses and I needed them. "Hey buddy, mate, get me your sunnies, give me your sunnies," I said. He just looked at me and said: "Mate, sunnies aren't going to help you. You need to just keep holding on."

They put me in the back of an ambulance. I remember feeling so hot and demanded air-conditioning. "Turn the air-conditioning on, it's hot! It's hot, it's hot! I'm burning, what's going on? Turn it on!" I was being pretty demanding but I was in so much pain that trying to get comfortable was my only priority. The medic was trying to calm me down. "Mate, it's OK. Stay calm, we're going to get you to the hospital," he said. They probably already had it on but I couldn't feel it at all, my skin was just so hot.

I can't remember how long the trip to the hospital was, but when we got there I was put on another stretcher. All of a sudden, people swarmed around me. They started cutting off the bandages that had been wrapped around me and cutting off my shorts.

There was a real sense of urgency now. I kept calling out: "What's going on?" But they ignored me. They were trying to find a vein and it was all commotion, a lot of noise and someone yelled out desperately: "I can't find a vein!"

All I could take in was a jumble of sounds and images. A mask came down over my face and I closed my eyes as they started to count down: "Five, four, three, you're going to be out in a moment." I felt a slice into the flesh in my groin. It didn't hurt. I just felt something. Then there was a pool of warm blood all over my groin, my leg, my waist. I could feel the warm blood running across my skin. That was the last thing I remember of my arrival back in Australia.

When I awoke I was on the move again. I was being taken to Adelaide because Perth hospitals could not cope with any more casualties. I was later told that it was then that Dr John Greenwood, from Royal Adelaide Hospital, came into the picture. He saw me on the tarmac and said: "He's coming with me, this guy here; I'm going to save him. He's coming with me."

I didn't wake up until I was in a small plane. I was strapped in pretty tight, ready to go. I had no idea what was going on. There were just snippets of sounds and scenes. Of doctors and nurses all huddled over me and all around me. Of noises from the medical equipment, just a steady "beep, beep, beep" from the machines.

I remember thinking I was one of two patients. I was stressing out. I tried to say something but couldn't talk. My throat was so sore from all the smoke I'd inhaled and jammed full of tubes. A doctor tried to reassure me. "It's OK, I'm going to help you, you're going to pull through, mate. Stay calm, I'm going to save you," he said. And then I was out of it again.

For a week or so I was in and out of consciousness. The first thing I remember about Adelaide is looking up and seeing my mum. She had on a hair net and was looking down at me and crying.

8

Crucified and mummified

Mum had that concerned mother look on her face. I wasn't sure whether I was awake or dreaming, and I kept thinking I was in heaven and my mum was an angel. I just started crying.

I couldn't really talk because of all the tubes and the damage and pain from the smoke. I was so burnt and wrapped up that she couldn't really do anything except touch my forehead and reassure me that everything was going to be OK.

I realised that I really was alive. But I knew I wasn't in a good state. And then I was out again. My life was basically about getting ready for or being treated after operations.

I was really confused about what had happened and would spend a lot of time crying, even sometimes when I wasn't exactly sure why. Every time I closed my eyes, even when I was awake, I could see it all again in my mind. I just couldn't get the images out of my head. I kept asking: "Why me, why do I have to go through this?"

Days after the bombings, I still had all the mud and dirt from Bali on my feet, and I had filthy black fingernails. I remember my mum cleaning my feet. Somewhere around 40 per cent to 50 per cent of my body had been badly burnt, with many more superficial burns on top of that.

Just about all of my back and the back of my arms had deep burns from falling back into the fire at the Sari Club. My legs were also badly burnt. The doctors had to take skin off the good parts of my body and "stretch" it out to cover a burnt area. They took skin off just about everywhere that I wasn't burnt. My thighs, my stomach, my shins, everywhere but my chest. At one stage they were toying with the idea of taking skin from my chest as well but my family said: "No, leave his chest." I think it was something that they believed was important to me and just wanted some part of me to look untouched. They were right – it's what I wanted too.

Preparation for the graft process was described to me as like putting sheets of pasta through a pasta press machine, which puts holes through it and stretches it out. It leaves some areas with a perforated look. I still have that on some parts of my arms. Dressing changes on the areas from where the grafts had been taken were shocking. The skin left was red raw and those dressing changes hurt more than those on the burns.

I was put into a "crucifix" position to help the healing. The grafts on my legs and arms were OK. They were bandaged. They weren't great but the grafts had taken. My back was not as good. I remember at every dressing change, and every time it came for an operation, my back was always an issue. They would tell me: "We don't have enough skin to cover it." Every time a graft failed, they had to scrape my skin almost to the bone and re-do it.

There was also a lot of infection, especially as my treatment had been delayed for so long while I waited in Bali. Every time I sat up you could see the slime and green muck that was continually oozing from my back. I was also losing a lot of blood and needed more than 40 blood transfusions. I was set in splints, "crucified" and "mummified", needing three dressing changes a day: morning, noon and night. It was excruciating, ripping my skin off every time with the bandages, and it felt like torture knowing that the routine of changes was relentless. I would argue with the nurses. "Why do you have to do it so much?"

There were a few scary moments in intensive care when I nearly lost my fight to survive, but one in particular sticks in my mind. After one of my operations, I went into hypothermia and was going in and out of consciousness. I could feel myself dying, I was so cold, I couldn't breathe and I was begging for someone to get my mum so I could say goodbye.

But when she got there, she started to stroke my head and talk to me. I managed to pull every bit of strength I had together to stay alive and she sat by my side reminding me to breathe, going through the martial arts breathing techniques that I'd shown her years before.

She told me there was no way in hell I was leaving. I wasn't allowed to go, not now, not after everything I'd fought for so far. I believed her and somehow managed to make it through that night. My martial arts training and the support from my mum pulled me back from the edge. Every day was a challenge but that was my biggest fight to stay alive.

As my back slowly started to heal, the nurses not only had to change the dressings, but also had to pull out the staples that held the grafts together on my back. Huge staples, and they had to use tweezers to pick them out one by one.

There were tubes in my mouth, my nose, my veins. After a while, I was able to administer my own pain relief. They tried to rig up a button on my hand but because my hands were so burnt, I couldn't press it. So they set up a special device with a piece of tubing attached to the pain-relief drugs. It hung about 5cm from my mouth. Whenever I wanted pain relief, I would lean up, put my lips on it like a straw and blow. The pressure would administer the pain relief. I was on a one-minute limit. Every minute, I was able to have more if I needed it. I counted down that minute so many times. I knew without even looking at a clock that I had 10 seconds left and I'd be on that thing again. And then sometimes if the pain was too bad, I was allowed to have more.

After a while, the doctors were concerned that I was using it for the wrong reasons – not just for pain relief but also to put myself to sleep and to deal with nightmares. In the morning, I would wake up from a drug-induced sleep and remember being told off quite a few times for using the drugs to put myself out. I found that not only did it relieve the physical pain but it also stopped me from thinking of the things that I wanted to get out of my head.

I couldn't use my hands to press a call button so I had a bell on a toe. I would ring it whenever I needed something. I'd ring it to change the channel on TV, or if I felt I had to go to the toilet. That was painful, going to the toilet, and totally demoralising as well. I needed help even to crap in a bedpan. And I was often frightened, having nightmares day and night, and so I rang that bell whenever I could.

I could never be awake much longer than half an hour before I was out of it again. I'd want to go to sleep. After every dressing change I'd be pretty worn out, the pain was unbearable. To calm down, I'd pump on that morphine until I drifted back off to sleep.

When I was conscious, I mostly tried to listen to music on a CD player. John Butler Trio was one of my favourites and they helped get me through. During my dressing changes, I used to listen to them but I could still feel the pain. The music just helped me cope with the worst parts and helped take my mind off the endless days filled with nothing but depression and despair.

I was angry. I was angry with everyone. I shouted at the doctors and nurses who were trying to help me, anyone and everyone who caused me pain. If someone bumped my arm I'd let them have it. I just tore strips off them. "How could you bump into me, how could you do that! It hurts, get out of here!"

I still felt thirsty constantly and for a long time was still only being allowed teaspoons of crushed ice. This felt unbelievably good. It's amazing what a difference something like that can make when you are desperate. And I was desperate.

9

A mother's view – hearing the news

I WAS ASLEEP AFTER HAVING AN EARLY NIGHT. I THINK it was about 4 am when the phone rang, and when I answered there was a woman on the other end of the line. She said: "Are you Jayne Britten, Phil Britten's mother?" I said: "Yes" and she said that a bomb had gone off.

It was Mira Stannard. I didn't have a clue who she was or what she was talking about, but she said: "We've got him, we've taken him to a clinic, here's our number, please ring us back if you need to."

She gave me a really long phone number and then I hung up and sat there for a minute and then I just lay down and went back to sleep. I just didn't function, it just didn't hit me. I didn't even think about what she'd said, I just blocked it out. Later I realised that it was my body's way of coping, to just shut it out. I must've thought it was part of a bad dream. What she was saying didn't happen in real life, not to me anyway.

I'm not an early riser but, for some reason, about 5 am I got up and turned the TV on and that's when I made the connection and the full force of what had happened hit me. This was not a dream. It was very, very real and my son was in real danger. Journalists started ringing and I just kept trying to call over and over again the number Mira had given me.

I must have written it down wrong because I just couldn't get through. Then a little bit later, the Kingsley Football Club coach, Simon Quayle, rang and said that, yes, there had been a bombing and that they were still looking for Philip. Then I heard nothing more for about another 12 hours, except for what was on the news. It was absolute agony to sit there and wait for news, not to know whether he was dead or alive.

Reporters kept calling so I got a girlfriend to come over. She was answering the phone for me because I didn't want to, but we needed to be available in case it was the club again, Mira or perhaps even Phil. I was just waiting for someone to tell me whether he was OK. We just didn't know what to think.

Simon had said they were going through the hospitals to try to find the boys. The hours just dragged on and on and on. I couldn't think about what might have happened. It was too much, too painful to let my imagination run away. I sat there numb and held on to hope. It was just such a horrific day.

Finally, I got the phone call I was waiting for with some news, and even better, it was Phil calling me himself. Someone had lent him a phone and Phil said: "I'm all right, everything's OK, don't worry, I'm alive, don't worry any more." I was so relieved. I could hear his voice and knew that he was alive, and that was all that mattered.

I didn't know the extent of his injuries at that stage. A volunteer from the hospital then rang me and said that he had been burnt and had shrapnel wounds, and that he would be evacuated as soon as possible.

By that time we had heard that they were being evacuated to various hospitals around the country. Phil was one of the last to be flown out. Someone rang me from Darwin, a doctor or a nurse, I'm not really sure who, and said he was on the tarmac waiting and he was going to Adelaide.

Phil's boss at the air-conditioning business rang and said: "We're booking you on the next flight to Adelaide. Don't worry about anything, there's a hotel room waiting for you when you get there." About 5 am the next day, I was on a flight over there.

When I got to Adelaide, Phil had already arrived. His boss had a driver waiting at the airport to look after us. We first went to the hotel room that they'd organised, dropped off our bags and then drove to Royal Adelaide Hospital.

When we got there Phil was in the intensive care unit. They let me go straight up to see him. He was connected to tubes everywhere and there were machines all around him. I took photos. Looking back it seems like a gory thing to do. I don't know why I took them. Maybe I thought it would be the last time I saw him, I don't know. He was in a pretty bad state.

I was just shocked. I had no idea he was going to be so bad. Even though I knew he was wounded, nothing could have prepared me for what I saw. And even then Phil would never let me hang around while the bandages were changed, never. So it was probably a couple of months before I actually saw the full extent of his injuries.

When he had bandage changes, he would always tell me to leave but I could still hear him scream. It was that painful. And it hurt me. My child was screaming out in pain and there was nothing I could do.

The first time I saw the severity of his burns was after his third lot of grafts. They had only lightly covered him, they hadn't bandaged him back up; the sheet slipped and that was the first time I saw the wounds. They were raw, weeping and excruciating. And they were almost all over his body.

I'll never forget what one of the nurses said to me one day: "You know, it's as if our country's gone to war. This is like a war zone, we're seeing casualties you'd see from the frontline." Usually it was house fires or other burns that they dealt with. She said this was a whole new thing for them as well, not just physically but also emotionally. These wounds were caused on purpose by other people, not just by accident. The medical team and especially the nurses were just amazing, amazing people.

10

Living in a nightmare

IT WASN'T UNTIL AFTER THE FIRST FEW DAYS IN Adelaide that I really became aware for the first time of exactly what had happened in Bali. My mum had the difficult job of making it clear to me that there had been a terrorist attack.

Early on, I was told seven of my mates were still missing, but there was still some hope that they were alive and maybe were at a hospital, but unidentifiable, as I'd been. I just kept hoping that they weren't going through what I was going through.

I was kept up to date with events as they unfolded, and gradually it became grimmer and grimmer and I had to accept the worst. It would be news like "They found an arm but that's all they've found", or "They found a wallet", things like that. It got more and more bleak as people's remains were sent home and the funerals started. It hurt so much inside, as I had to take it all in and I wanted to be at everyone's funerals but couldn't. I was still just barely surviving myself and had to focus on that. At least I knew they weren't in any more pain.

I had a good support network in Adelaide. My mum stayed the whole time and other members of my immediate family came and went. Ben Clohessy and Simon Quayle flew to Adelaide to help boost my spirits, and to reassure me that all the boys and families back in Perth were doing the best they could with the situation. They said although there was a lot to cope with and so many funerals, everyone was sticking together.

I felt really, really devastated and I was really down. I was also angry at where I was. I would ask: "Why couldn't I have just lost my leg? Just, bang, take my leg and it's over, I'm not in this much pain, this ongoing pain, I can't take it any more!" And sometimes I just thought it would have been so much easier for me and everyone if I'd just died. I wished I had given in back in Bali and let myself die. Why did I have to fight? I could have had a funeral and just have left it at that.

I thought: "What kind of life do I have left now, the state that I'm in?" I'd seen myself in mirrors by now and had no clear idea of what the outcome would be when I'd "healed". All I could see ahead was me being a scary-looking freak, burnt with no teeth, bloodied, swollen and a head full of nightmares and memories of people dying all around me. That was my future. No end goal was in sight. I couldn't see how it would be any better than that.

I went through so many different moods and couldn't handle reminders of what I'd been through and seen. If the news came on TV and was about terrorism, I had to have it turned off immediately. I couldn't watch any of it. And then there were the terrible nightmares. I felt I couldn't escape.

One of my nightmares was like I was in a war zone. It was similar to a typical movie about World War II or the Vietnam War, except I felt, smelt and experienced it all as if I were there. I don't know whether I was actually awake and hallucinating or asleep and dreaming. I was still in intensive care and in such a bad way that there was always a nurse sitting by my door.

One time she walked off and didn't come back for a while and I started to see smoke drifting past the door and then saw the faint red glow of a fire coming towards me. The flames and smoke started to increase and I started to hear "fft fft fft fft fft fft fft", the sound of helicopter blades and people screaming. It was just like the bombing all over again but I was trapped, with all these tubes coming out of me, strapped onto a bed and couldn't get out. I imagined people were being dropped off by the helicopter into the hospital, people being taken out by the chopper and big explosions nearby. There were no guns going off, just lots of bombs, and the people were getting closer and closer to my door. I could see the flames and would try to yell out but no one could hear me. I finally thought to myself: "I've got to get out of here. If I don't I'm going to get burnt again just like in the Sari Club." And then I came to, screaming and panicking until they sedated me again and I finally settled.

I had that sort of dream a lot. I often dreamed of something being on fire and it was hard to take, hard to close my eyes to sleep because, although I was now safe, I had no escape from what I saw in my head.

I felt so repulsed by myself. I was dirty, dishevelled and burnt. I'd always taken pride in my appearance and now I couldn't even stand to see my own reflection. At one point, they put a young, pretty nurse on to look after me. She just came in and carried on like there was nothing wrong with me at all and it did help a little. It was a deliberate move by the hospital staff, and it made me feel normal again, like a young guy in his 20s, just chatting to another person my own age. For a moment, I felt just that little bit better about myself.

I loved having my mum there. Sometimes I'd get really angry with her and yell at her, but I loved having her there. She was just so full of love for me that she took whatever I threw at her and stayed by my side. A bit later, my stepfather Wim and my brother Ash came over to Adelaide. Ash was only 13, and when he came into the room, he saw me, turned to go out again and fainted. He just couldn't handle it and when I was told he'd gone down like that, I didn't know what to do.

He came around again and we just laughed and I said: "Dork!" He found it very hard to see me the way that I was. When he went out of the room, I said to my mum: "I hate it when people react like that when they see me." I didn't realise that he'd heard me say that.

I didn't know how tough it was on him until later. I had no idea how much it meant to him to be there for me and to stay by my side. My kid brother was so desperate to grow up at that moment and be there for me, and I love him so much for that. He was only able to stay for a short while and he fought to be able to stay longer, but in the end he had to go back to Perth, back to school, and just wait for me there.

Dr Greenwood was still in charge of my treatment. I never saw him much because he would do the operations and then just do his checks once or twice a day. He would always come in with a group of people — a physio, a nurse, it was like a viewing gallery. He would arrive with them, update them and instruct them on what was going to happen next. He'd check out how I was feeling and then would be gone again — next room, next patient.

There were some little things I looked forward to. Burns milkshakes were one thing. They were a sort of protein shake designed to deliver energy, and they were a real treat as they tasted like McDonald's thickshakes. It wasn't the sort of thing I was expecting in a hospital.

Another thing that helped were all the messages of support I got. I've still got boxes full of postcards, letters and drawings from primary school kids. Letters said things such as: "I hope you get better soon so you can come back and play for Kingsley Football Club, stay strong." It would be from a six-year-old kid and would have a little squiggly picture on it.

Every day or every few days, there'd be another big bag of postcards and letters. Mum would read them to me and hold them up so I could see them. It helped. I had them pinned on the walls and they would bring a smile to my face. The messages were so genuine and innocent that they really touched me and made a world of difference to my otherwise bleak days.

I was sent a video by the guys at martial arts, even though I hadn't been down there for some time because I'd been focusing on football. It was motivating but also a bit upsetting. Some big names in the sports world got in touch with me too.

The first time I heard from a sporting star was when I was being taken to have my first shower since the bombing. I hadn't got out of my bed at this stage so it was quite a big moment. They carried me in my sheet, put me on a shower bed and I was naked, lying there feeling pretty bad about myself. It was the first time I'd been without bandages on and could see my skin, all purple, black and bloodied. It was the first time I'd actually seen the extent of the injuries to my whole body. It looked as if my legs were going to fall off; they were so purple and mangled. The nurses were rolling me over and it was just agony. Just as they started to pat me down to dry me, I was told someone was calling for me on the phone. I was pissed off! I thought: "No one's going to call me now, I'm having a shower, just take a message!" I said angrily: "Who is it?" The nurses said it was Jeff Fenech and Danny Green – two Australian champion boxers.

I wasn't really switched on to what was happening. Of course, I knew who they were. They were legends in the boxing world, but I didn't really register the names. I just said, "Take a message", and carried on being dried. When I got back to my room, they were actually waiting on the line! I found out that Danny Green had caught up with the boys who'd survived at the football club and for one of his fights he entered the ring wearing a Kingsley jumper in a show of support. And now here he was on the phone wanting to speak to me! He told me: "Well done, mate, you'll do well. Stay strong and don't give up. You're strong, you're a fighter and you've got your martial arts to help you. We're all here for you." Then Jeff Fenech got on the phone and had a chat to me as well, and I was so taken aback by it all, a bit bewildered about why they'd called me. I didn't know my progress was making news both in Perth and nationally. But it all helped, more than I think any of them knew.

11

The long road home

SLOWLY, BIT BY BIT, I STARTED TO IMPROVE. ONE OF the early challenges was to get my hands moving again, to be able to open and close them and move my fingers, something I hadn't been able to do for some time. My hands were so stiff from the burns that I still wasn't able to press the call button for the nurse.

The first phase was to get me to the point where I'd be able to use the call button, get the bell ringer off my toes and remove the tube, which I was still using to give myself pain-relief drugs. The day I was able to push the call button for the nurse was the day that I realised I could win this fight. Mentally it was a huge step forward for me.

After I'd achieved those goals, and once I was moved out of the crucifix position, I also had to try to sit up and then to stay sitting unassisted. I'd been lying flat on my back for about a month and had lost all my muscle strength. At first, just to sit up, I needed help. I'd get dizzy straight away and almost pass out and fall back down again. It was frustrating and emotionally draining every time.

Then it came time for me to be able to get off the bed. In the early stages, even small movements were really painful but I had to keep going. At this point, my physio was still coming in once a day to see how I was going and it was up to me to work on the exercises I was given, such as moving my hands or sitting up whenever I could get the strength to give it a go.

At the start, it didn't go well. I was still really depressed and didn't like always being told what to do. I didn't like all these people who'd been forced into my life. I was filled with hate for the whole world. It wasn't really until I thought seriously about going home that I began to get motivated to do better. They said to me: "We can't let you go home unless you can show us that you can get up and walk a lap of the corridor unassisted."

Right there and then, I had a goal to work towards, and if I wanted to go home I knew exactly what I had to do. And I really wanted to go home, to see my friends and the rest of my family.

After getting up off my back came moving to sit in a chair. I remember the first time I did that and have since seen a photo of it. I look pretty pissed off! I was in so much pain. I felt light-headed and annoyed that I was an invalid, barely able to move. And deep down I was burning with rage that someone had done this to me deliberately.

The pain was always there but next came trying to walk. The first steps were with a walking frame and a nurse or physio alongside me. It was just as you see with the elderly: a walking frame and me hobbling up to it and then two steps along. Two steps that was it.

I kept having a go and each time I got a little further, a little better, and then the next thing I was walking very gingerly on my own. Then came the time for me to put myself to the test to show them I could go home. I remember doing it. My mum was there, walking behind me, ready to catch me if I fell as I did a lap of the corridor. It was no more than 15 to 20 metres but it was a marathon for me. It took me a good five minutes or so, going really slowly, one step, two steps, stop; another step or, if I was feeling dizzy, I'd grab my mum to steady myself. She tried to help me by not grabbing me back, and saying: "C'mon Phil, you can do it, you're almost there." It felt like one step forward, two steps backwards.

We take walking for granted. I guess you take everything for granted until it's taken away from you. It was so frustrating knowing that less than two months earlier I was taking marks, kicking a footy, strong and fit, and now here I was, not even able to walk and starting all over again. It was really hard to deal with mentally as well as physically. But I was sick of being the "victim" and determined to overcome whatever was thrown at me.

When I was finally ready to go home, I had one more delay. I was in the same hospital as Peter Hughes, another guy from Perth who'd been in the bombing. The nurses came to me and said: "Peter's going home too but in a few days. We're going to fly you both out together so you'll have to wait just a little bit longer." I said it was OK by me, and in a few days we were ready to leave together.

I came out of the hospital on a stretcher. I was put into an ambulance and then into a wheelchair and loaded on the plane before the rest of the passengers.

I went up on a lift and couldn't use the wheelchair in the plane's aisle, so I had to walk gingerly and slowly to my seat.

I flew business class. I needed the room because of my injuries, and a nurse was by my side for the whole flight. She made sure that medically I was OK, but also psychologically that I was coping with the journey. I was still on heavy painkillers but any knock or bump would hurt. Any minor turbulence that's usually just a minimal inconvenience to a normal passenger was excruciating for me, so the whole plane ride was really difficult.

My hands had healed enough to enable me to wear a hand pressure garment, but the rest of me was still bandaged tightly. When I arrived in Perth, there was a media circus at the airport: "The last of the Kingsley football players was arriving home!" I'd known by then that the Bali bombing was a big deal to the media but I hadn't had to deal with any of it directly before this. It was pretty intimidating and I felt angry, as if I were being gawked at all over again. I was pushed out in my wheelchair, past the cameras and quickly into the privacy of a waiting ambulance.

The ambulance took me straight to Royal Perth Hospital (RPH) and while the whole time I was in

Adelaide, I'd wanted to be home in Perth, now I was here, I just wanted to be back in Adelaide. I was surrounded once again by strangers and felt almost homesick for what I'd left behind. I knew there were a lot of people who wanted to see me but I wanted some quiet time by myself first. I wasn't ready for visitors.

As soon as I got to RPH, I was whisked up to the burns unit, had to strip off naked and was showered because of the infection risk. A lady came in to scrub me down. It was humiliating: being scrubbed down all the time, looking at myself and my burns. I looked disgusting and now had a stranger washing me down, washing my groin and private parts. I felt like I'd hit a new low point. I got out of the shower and I was patted down and put into a backless hospital gown in a room with Peter Hughes. Although we'd been in the Adelaide burns unit, which is a quarantine area, we had to be quarantined again in Perth. Infection on a burns ward can quickly become a death sentence.

I lay there wishing I was back in Adelaide, back with the nurses who knew who I was, who'd looked after me and made me comfortable. Perth was, by contrast, a lot more regimented.

I soon met my physiotherapist, Dale Edgar. There were times when I hated him with a passion, but looking back, what he did for me was nothing short of a miracle. As soon as I arrived, they began work on getting me moving. It wasn't just physical, it was getting me motivated mentally as well. At my first meeting with Dale, he said: "Right, we're getting you up and about and I'm getting you into the gym."

I thought: "How am I going to do this? I can barely walk, let alone do exercises in a gym!" My first impression was "I just hate this guy." After showering and being re-bandaged and dressed, I lay back down in bed feeling miserable. I started to look forward to my dinner and getting the evening's pain relief.

A woman came in with my meal and Dale was standing at the door. She started to walk towards me with the tray and Dale said: "No, wait, leave it at the door. If you want your dinner, you come over here and get it." I looked at him and thought: "What the fuck are you doing? You sadistic bastard!" I was so used to getting it all given to me, being sat up, having my pillows adjusted and being constantly asked: "Is everything OK? How are you feeling?"

Now I'd arrived in Perth and here was Dale saying: "If you want dinner, come and get it, get moving, let's do it!" I just left it there for a good 10 to 15 minutes, but eventually I got hungry and had to walk over and get it. I didn't see him but I knew he was thinking: "He's going to get up and get it." And that was my first interaction with Dale. I had other physios who helped me along the way too, but he's the one whom I remember the most, the one who'd managed to get through to me and really pushed me always to try harder.

I was now being cared for by Dr Fiona Wood, who knew Dr Greenwood, my specialist back in Adelaide. Dr Wood came in and assessed me. For the moment, I didn't need any more operations, but I still had open wounds that needed attention. It was agreed that I didn't need any more skin grafting and that the problem areas would eventually now heal, given proper care and attention.

My treatment in Perth revolved around monitoring my pain and undergoing intense physiotherapy to get me moving again. During that time I had a lot of visitors. It was really difficult to cope with. It was hard for me and it was hard for my friends to see how I was. They remembered how I was before the bombing and were always shocked to see me when they walked in. Physically, I was just a shadow of the person I used to be.

I just lay there while they visited. I had no muscle tone, missing teeth and many of my burns exposed, and I was just generally really scruffy. I'd lost so much weight and was looking scarily thin. I remember one of my friends came to see me and just sat there and cried, saying: "Why do people do this sort of thing?"

I was meant to be in Royal Perth for quite some time and was then expected to move to Shenton Park Rehabilitation Centre, but I'd made up my mind that I was getting better and going straight home. To get out of Royal Perth, I had to show them I could manage at home. So again, I had tasks to accomplish. This time it was in the gym. At first, it was just getting on an exercise bike. To begin with, every turn of the pedal was painful, but I pushed through and it got better as I went along.

Then there were some weights to rebuild my muscle strength. I was still really stiff under the arms. I still couldn't reach my face with my own hands, couldn't brush my teeth or touch my nose but as I kept at it the skin began to stretch out. And it was then I was allowed to go home.

I'd been in Royal Perth Hospital for only a week.

12

A mother's view – bedside vigil

I stayed in Adelaide the whole time Phil was there, about a month. The Red Cross got me a long-term hotel room and so I went to the hospital in the morning and then back in the afternoon until Phil asked me to go.

We had to stay positive. We couldn't think anything else. We knew that he would come through. Anything else just wasn't an option. I believed that if Phil wasn't meant to make it, he wouldn't have made it out of the Sari Club in the first place.

It was courage and strength that got him over that wall and out of the club and that's exactly what he needed to keep fighting in the hospitals. He got serious infections and three times they had to go back in, strip everything right back to the bone and re-graft.

There was one truly scary time that they rang me and told me to get there NOW! Phil was struggling after his third operation and had asked to see me. He'd gone into shock, he was just shaking and all this horrible stuff was dripping off the table. I then saw the horrific wounds. That was the only time that he really scared me, but I thought "No" and refused to believe he would give up. I just told him that he had to live, that he wasn't allowed to die. You know, be strong, push through it, breathe through it, you're not allowed to leave now, not after all this. We sat there and breathed together, as he'd been taught in martial arts. We just focused on him keeping breathing and staying with me. And, thank God, he did it, he made it.

I've met parents who lost their children in Bali. They were often relieved that their child went quickly because they knew what Phil had gone through and didn't know whether they could bear to watch it, especially as just making it to this point didn't guarantee that they would still survive. There were so many who didn't, who died in the hospitals, who'd suffered.

I think that sometimes Phil felt like he had to look after me. He'd lie there while I'm crying and he's saying: "Calm down, mum, it's all right," which is just him. He's been giving me lessons in life from a very young age.

In some ways, Phil really isolated himself: he was silently very determined to go through this. But there were letters from children, which really helped, and he was also getting postcards from schools. A lot of support was organised by Phil's martial arts instructor. He'd send postcards and videos just to cheer Phil up.

There was a particular time when they sent in a very pretty nurse about his age. He was so embarrassed for anyone to see him like he was but she came in and just talked to him like he was a normal guy, the same age as her, not some guy lying there in bed terribly burnt. I think that helped a bit. It made him feel normal again, just for a moment.

Phil never complained to me about any of it, except once, about the food. He'd be angry at times, which was expected, and he would get frustrated, but he never complained. He just got on with things.

I eventually came home with Phil on the same flight from Adelaide. I wasn't going to let him out of my sight.

In a way, I sort of got cut loose once we got back to Perth. You're only allowed a certain number of visitors in the intensive care ward because of the danger of infection and there were so many people in Perth who wanted to see him now he was back. A few of his good mates took over his bedside and I finally had to let go. I had to allow him to start being independent again. So it was very rare that I'd see him once he got back to Perth. That was hard for me to adjust to after being there 24/7 but it was important that his normal life start to come back.

Phil really didn't talk to me a lot about what he was going through. He didn't talk to anyone about it. At times, I saw him really, really depressed and I was really worried about him. You could just see it in his face. It was a mental thing because he faced every single physical challenge that came in front of him. That's Phil; he doesn't want anything beating him. He puts challenges on himself, but you can't always control the mind.

13

Dale Edgar – RPH Physiotherapist

Dale Edgar was in charge of the physiotherapy program at the burns unit at Royal Perth Hospital when Phil returned to Perth.

A LARGE BURN INJURY WITH A SHOULDER PROBLEM IS a difficult rehab prospect. Hands and shoulders are probably the most difficult areas of the body after grafts because of the need for flexibility and the thin skin, and Phil had a nasty scar developing on the back of his shoulder.

The patients we saw from Bali were mostly young people, and most of them who came in the door were slightly different to our normal patients who don't necessarily have the drive to get better. These guys were just in the wrong place at the wrong time. It was something that happened to them by accident, and that changes where your mind is.

But when I first saw Phil it was hard to talk to him. I didn't get the feeling that he was really into getting up and getting moving. I realised that the reason that these guys hadn't got up was because they had spent some time in intensive care.

We had a little bit of reassignment of attitude to be done because we are, as a team, very much about getting people moving. So, you don't sit in bed, you get up and go to the toilet. You don't sit in bed and have your food, you get up and sit in a chair like a normal person.

Our first real challenge was to get him on board and to start to get him doing the things that he needed to do for his rehab when he wasn't in front of a physio. I can push someone and get amazing things done when I am there, but that doesn't produce a good post-burn outcome in my opinion.

What produces a good post-burn outcome is someone who can do what they need to do when I am not around. I guess Phil was angry, as he had a right to be. He had to go through the grieving process.

But he also had the attitude of a young semi-elite football player, and thankfully in the end we could use that in his favour. I basically told him how it was. You convince people and educate people as to how they are going to get the best result.

We set up a fit ball, exercises with weights and resistance, balance exercises; these guys had injuries on various parts of their bodies so they all required input into all of their systems. We do a lot of work in front of mirrors because when you get burnt you have damaged the peripheral nerve field and lost your position sense. You basically lose your body's perception of where that limb is.

Very quickly you have to get people to understand that there will be pain with movement, but it's not doing any damage. I don't know how many times a day I will say: "You are not damaging your burn when you get moving." That is the fear that stops people moving. It is the anxiety that they will do some damage to the wounds or to their grafts.

They develop fear avoidance strategies that include anger, pushing people away, telling the physio to piss off, telling the nurse "Bugger off I am going to have a pee in the bed". To these guys' credit they very quickly picked up "OK, these RPH guys mean business. They are working towards getting the best outcome for us and making sure we get out the other side again".

The other thing that I think was unique to the Bali group, and this worked brilliantly for Phil, was that there were about eight to 10 of them who regularly came into the gym. Phil and one or two others were the primary catalysts. There was a lot of camaraderie about that group.

Phil was one of the core people in the group who supported others in terms of "It's OK, let's get on with it". For a physio, it was fantastic. You set them up on different bits of exercise equipment and you get them moving around. They were obviously enjoying it and supporting each other. When one would have a down day somebody would come over to support them. You could see it happening. It was a different situation to what we had expected in the burns unit, and we have learned from this and try to emulate that now.

We will set up the gym and we will have multiple patients in there and you get this banter between patients. They will say "Oh you have a burn there", and "That must be bad", or "That must be painful", and the other person will say "Not really, I am getting on with it".

So instead of it being me saying "You will get over this and you need to get on with it", you will have other patients who will start to mould that mind-set. I noticed Phil turning around very quickly because

ABOVE
A young Phil with
baby brother Ash.

LEFT
Phil (front left) was
an up-and-coming
football star
with West Perth
Football Club.

ABOVE
Phil (2nd from right) and the Kingsley Football
Club 'Cats' outside Perth International Airport.

BELOW
Dinner at Bagus Bar, Kuta, Bali.

RIGHT
A photo of Phil escaping the Sari Club.
This photo is from a page of *New Idea* magazine.

This image of Philip is so powerful, but also sparked complaints when we ran it. Philip encouraged its use again here to highlight the atrocity.

ABOVE
The street was littered with burnt out cars.
Image courtesy Barry Baker, *The West Australian*.

BELOW
The massive 700kg bomb left behind a tangled
mess of destruction and debris.

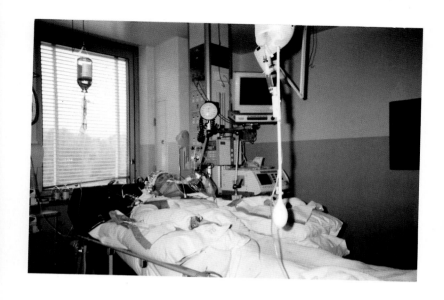

ABOVE
Phil's burns injuries put him in a critical condition.

BELOW
To prevent his skin from fusing, he was strapped
down in a 'crucifix' position.

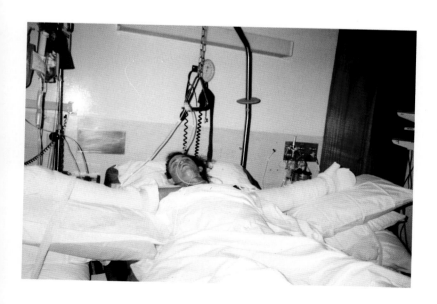

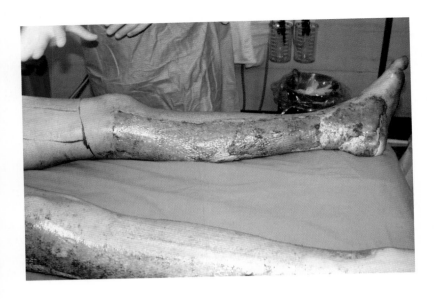

ABOVE
Phil needed numerous skin grafting operations.

BELOW
The worst of his injuries were on his legs and back.

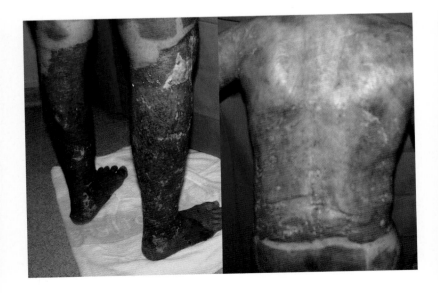

ABOVE
Phil's mother, Jayne, coordinated his recovery
and liaised with family and friends back in Perth.

BELOW
Jayne remained by his side in Adelaide.

Phil sitting up
for the first time,
still fed by a
nasogastric tube.

Phil needed to
be able to walk
the length of the
hospital corridor
before he could
return to Perth.

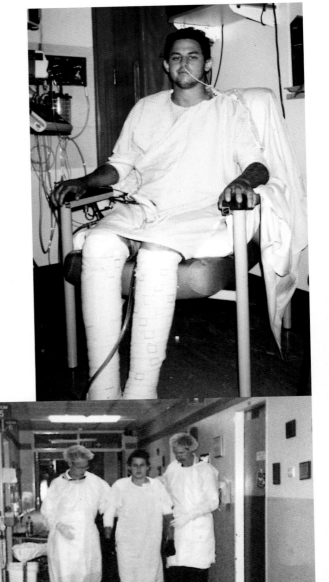

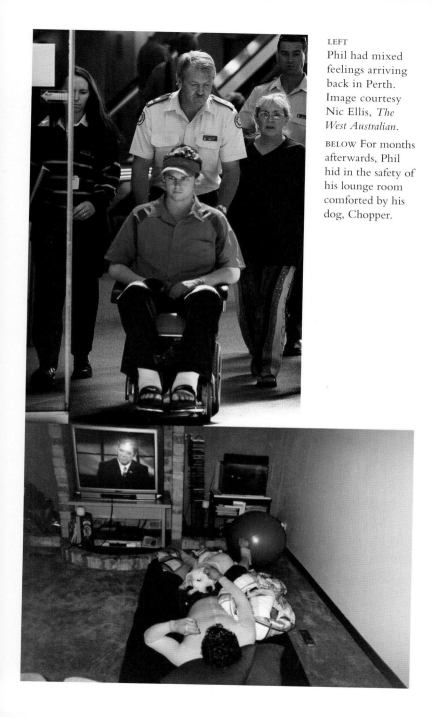

LEFT
Phil had mixed feelings arriving back in Perth. Image courtesy Nic Ellis, *The West Australian*.

BELOW For months afterwards, Phil hid in the safety of his lounge room comforted by his dog, Chopper.

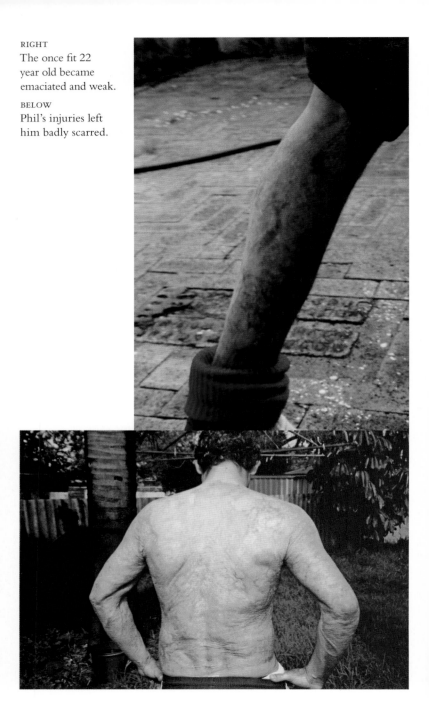

RIGHT
The once fit 22 year old became emaciated and weak.

BELOW
Phil's injuries left him badly scarred.

ABOVE
The start of the 2003 football season was bittersweet for Phil.

BELOW
Less than six months after the bombing, Phil had his
comeback game for Kingsley Football Club.

ABOVE
Phil and his rescuers, Mira, Tansen and Sai.

BELOW
Reuniting with the Bali Clinic nurse and the
driver who took him to Sanglah Hospital.

Phil paid his respects at the first anniversary in Bali.

Former prime minister John Howard also attended
the first anniversary service in Bali.

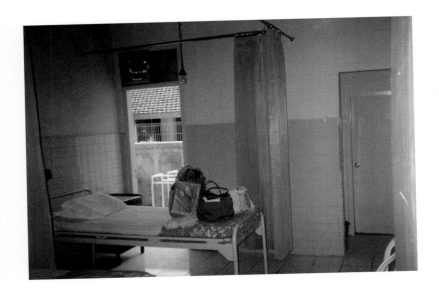

ABOVE
A room at Sanglah Hospital, similar to the one
Phil was placed in upon his arrival.

BELOW
Meeting Prince Charles with Fiona Wood A.M.
in 2005 at Royal Perth Hospital.
Image courtesy Greg Burke, *The West Australian*.

After the bombing, Phil decided to start living life to the full.

Phil's first full-contact Muay Thai fight in 2007.
He won by a second round knock out.

ABOVE Phil now owns a successful martial arts business.
Image courtesy Michael O'Brien, *The West Australian*.

BELOW
Phil and wife Rebecca in 2012 with their two boys –
Benjamin and new baby Riley.
Image courtesy Lincoln Baker, *The West Australian*.

I think we tapped into something that was very comfortable for him as a guy who had regularly done physical activity.

As soon as we convinced Phil that it wasn't going to do him damage, he was away. The way that he pushed himself in that gym as an outpatient, I don't think any of the others got to that level. Phil had to work hard. He had trunk burns, shoulder burns, arm burns, so he had to think about "What happens when I add all of that scar together, how do I get my full movement back?"

Right back then we were saying: "You are going back to footy, what do you need to do when you go back to footy?" He would say: "I need to have both hands above my head taking a mark." So we said "OK, that's where we are going," and we would set those goals up.

We could also say: "Right, if you are going back to footy you need to be able to bump, you need to be able to run." So we could do balance exercises, strengthening exercises, get them on their tummy over a fit ball; that's a brilliant exercise for someone who has been stuck in bed, particularly someone who has been in ICU because that's where all of your trunk muscles go to sleep.

You need to restore that if you are going to get your core stability back and if you are going to get the ability to get your arms above your head with strength. Phil took that on with gusto. I don't think I have ever seen anyone else take on the sideways fitball stretch with the same gusto. Phil went hell for leather on that one because he knew if he could get his full movement back in all that scar, from hip right through to fingertip he would be able to play footy again.

He came in every day and he would hit it hard. To his credit that's probably what got him to this point now. He did the hard work early and he got himself strong. I think that's what led him down the track of martial arts because that is about flexibility and strength.

He had come a long way in terms of his rehab when he got to us; he was probably five out of 10 at that stage, he was about half way there. Now he is probably close to 10 out of 10 in terms of outcome. In my whole career, there are probably only two or three people who have got an outcome that you would compare to Phil's.

14

Day in day out

ABOUT SIX WEEKS AFTER THE BOMBINGS I WENT HOME
to my house in Koondoola, which I'd bought two
years earlier. People offered to let me stay with them
so they could help me, but I just wanted to go home.

When I arrived back at my house, it was an amazing
sight. While I'd been in hospital, my cousin Adam
had got together a heap of his mates and had repainted
and put in new carpets and blinds. My workplace,
Direct Engineering Services, had installed a brand
new ducted air-conditioning system. They all went
above and beyond to make sure I had something nice
to come home to, and that I would be comfortable
in the heat of summer. It was incredible and I've

never forgotten all the generosity and kindness when I needed it most.

The air-conditioning really saved me as summer started to heat up. Perth has intense hot weather and we used to keep the house as dark as we could to keep it as cool as possible. But after the initial lift to my mood when I arrived home and saw how much everyone cared, I quickly sank into a dark depression once again.

I'd been really looking forward to seeing my dog Chopper again, but when I walked in, he didn't recognise me because of the pressure garments and hospital smell. I went over to him and he started growling and barking at me. It broke my heart and I thought: "My dog doesn't even know who I am." It took him a while but he started to realise that it really was me and became even more loyal than before, as if he knew I really needed a friend.

During this time my friends really rallied around me, especially Garth Allen, who'd spent a lot of time by my bedside in Royal Perth Hospital. He organised a local quiz night fundraiser, which was aimed at helping to support me financially and to buy a car with power steering and air-conditioning, which I'd need to be independent. My mobility problems and burns meant my old open-top 4WD wouldn't cut it any more once I was able to drive.

The Red Cross also provided some financial assistance and a lot of bills were deferred through good will, such as my mortgage repayments and utilities expenses. Balimed was a fund set up by the Australian government, which guaranteed full coverage of all Bali-related medical expenses. The government also wiped my student loans and immediate tax obligations to help me get back on my feet financially once I was better. But in the meantime, I just had to make do for a while on social security benefits for day-to-day living.

My routine was the same, day after day. I spent day and night in my hot, tight pressure suit to help my burns heal as smoothly as possible, with the air-conditioning turned up full. The pressure suit was from neck to toe. Then my gloves came over it as well. The gloves were fingerless so my toes, fingers and head were the only exposed parts of my body. And there was a small gap so I could go to the toilet.

I'd sleep in the lounge room on a mattress and basically lived there. I'd wake and then really carefully get up, go to the toilet and then back to the lounge room until the nurse arrived. She'd come in and we'd peel off the pressure suit, which would take about

15 minutes. Peeling it off was excruciating, like taking off a Band-Aid every day. I'd stand up and the nurse would start to slowly peel it down, bit by bit. I also still had some bandages underneath the pressure suit on my open wounds.

My skin was like leather, just like crocodile skin with no elasticity. It's a lot more flexible now. But back then, when the pressure suit came off, I'd walk like a stiff robot towards the shower and the nurse would have to watch while I showered in case I passed out or needed help. I had hospital-grade soap and any areas that I couldn't reach, the nurse would do. Some of the bandages on my open wounds wouldn't come off easily. The nurse would have to squeeze a special solution over the bandages, and with the water running over them she'd quickly rip them off. Even though I knew it was coming, I'd often scream in pain.

There were bits of bandage like that all over my body. So it was a real effort to care for my injuries. Washing hurt, towelling-off hurt, everything hurt. Once I was out of the shower, we'd have to start applying lanolin cream. We'd rub it all over my whole body. It was thick and really oily but would help keep moisture in my skin and stop me from seizing up as I healed.

Then the pressure suit went back on. It zipped up at the front. I'd step into it and then put my arms in. I still needed help for the most basic of daily tasks, including just zipping up my pressure suit, because although I could use my hands a little, they still weren't working very well and all I could do was fumble. The whole process took about an hour from start to finish.

After that, I'd set off for Royal Perth Hospital to do my physio at the gym every morning, seven days a week. They were all great people and even though I know it's their job, they were amazing to put up with patients like me and how I was behaving at the time. I was so miserable and still wishing that I'd just died back in Bali rather than having to face my life and the future I believed I had. There was just no end in sight for what I was going through.

As soon as I got home from the day's session, I'd just get back onto my mattress in the lounge room and that's pretty much where I'd stay for the rest of the day. I'd only get up to go to the toilet and get some food, and the rest of the time was spent watching movies or sleeping.

I didn't want any sunlight around me. I just hated it and had been told to stay out of the sun anyway because it obviously wasn't good for my injuries. It felt so hot, smouldering, and my skin felt as if it was badly sunburnt all the time – a type of sunburn that just wouldn't go away.

I was angry and depressed. I used to lie there and think: "Look at me, who's going to want me?" I'd always taken pride in my appearance and stayed really fit before Bali, but now I looked like shit. I felt like a freak. I was shattered inside every time I looked at the scars all over my arms, legs, back and chest. All I wanted to do was stay at home and survive each day.

I longed for simple things like going into the ocean again, but just going to the beach was an impossible dream. I still had to hide from the sun every day.

My girlfriend and I were still together but had grown apart since I came home from Adelaide. She still had to live her life and needed to move on with it. It wasn't long before she'd met someone else, and we broke up.

The nurse routine went on for the next 18 months or so and as we progressed, we began to phase it out slowly. Over time the nurses' visits were dropped back to every couple of days. Eventually the physio would also drop off a bit, but for the moment it was every day, with setbacks along the way to overcome.

There were, however, memorable moments that often boosted the spirits of those of us in the burns unit, and gave us something to look forward to. One time Johnnie Walker arranged for golf pro Robert Allenby and rugby union star Michael Lynagh to visit us at the physio rooms while the Johnnie Walker Classic golf tournament was held.

Another time, Prince Charles toured the burns unit, and we were invited to meet him. He spent a bit of time with each of us and you could tell that he genuinely wanted to know how we were recovering. He spoke with me for quite some time and we talked about what had happened in Bali, the effect it had on the island and also about loss in general. It was pretty relaxed I just sat on a fit ball and he sat alongside me, leaning in, listening to what I had to say. He was a pretty good guy and it was moments like that, when public figures wanted to know how we were going and took the time to lift us up, which helped break up the drudgery of each day. It made me feel special each time, even if just for a few moments. But soon after, it was back to the daily grind and hard work of physio once again.

Part of my treatment was designed to get my skin moving and stretching again. We had measurements on the walls and I would have to lean over like cricketer Merv Hughes used to do to limber up. At times the physio would also put his knee on my hip to stabilise me and put his hand on my elbow and push me to make me stretch. My skin was so tight, I couldn't brush my teeth or even touch my head.

One time, the physio was pushing and we were counting it out: "One, two, three, relax." Then he'd push me further and all of a sudden my skin just went "Snap!" The skin under my arm had split open. I said: "What was that?" He just said: "There's a little bit of blood, you've had a bit of a tear, no big deal." It was actually about the width of a 50-cent piece and the length of my armpit. So we had to stop, get the pressure suit off and deal with the tear instead of exercising that day.

So it was often a catch-22 situation. You wanted to stretch out as far as you could and coax your skin to give, but if you went too far you'd snap your skin and have to wait for it to heal before you could begin again. Another step forward, two steps back.

But I did start to feel fitter. I was hitting the treadmill, starting to do light weights and eating normal food, even starting to become a little chubby. And it was then that I decided to play football again.

15

Lacing the boots back up

Winter was approaching and the 2003 footy season was about to start. Everyone was telling me to let go of the idea of playing football again, to just give it up. But I couldn't.

I started to go down to Kingsley, watching the games and training with the team. Just having a football in my gloved hands was an amazing feeling. I was working really hard in the gym as part of my physio and had thought: "What's the harm in running around?" I might not play, but I could start training at least.

The doctors didn't know about it at first. I didn't tell them that I was going to go back to playing football. I didn't even really know myself that I was going to go back and play. Once the doctors found out, they said: "Do what you can do but don't push it too hard, because if you fall, you can scratch your skin and it'll open back up again." So I trained in a top-to-toe pressure suit and was careful.

It felt unbelievable to get the boots on again. Just to start trying to do things that I used to do was amazing, it felt liberating. Things started to change for me inside as well. I had a strong feeling that I needed to get back to the way that I was. I wanted to see whether I could do it, not to prove it to anyone but me; to say: "I can do this, I can be me again. I might not look the same, people might look at me and see a different person, but at least I'll be able to do the same things."

At Kingsley's first game of the season I led the team out onto the field, even though I still wasn't able to play. My rescuers, Mira, Tansen and Sai, had also been flown over from Bali by *New Idea* magazine that same weekend to be reunited with me. I felt I was meeting them for the first time, and really, I was.

The last time they'd seen me was when I left the clinic in Bali, bloodied and screaming in pain. Now I was just so excited to see them again, to introduce them to the real me and thank them for saving my life. There was this instant connection that I had with them, almost like a deep trust and love, that they were somehow now a part of my own family. I still call them my "second family".

During the season, former West Coast Eagles AFL player Adrian Barich, who worked in the media, came down to train with us one day. I was training in my full burns pressure suit and we had a friendly training match. Adrian and I were on opposing teams and we were playing on each other.

My feet always gave me problems, cracking and bleeding under the smallest amount of pressure. At one point during the game I sat down and took off a boot and it was full of blood. Adrian looked down and said: "Mate, are you all right?" I said: "Yep, no worries," wiped it out, laced the boot back up and got back on the field.

The next day, people said to me: "I heard someone talking about you on the radio." Apparently, Adrian was talking about his session at the Kingsley Football Club and what we'd gone through as a team in Bali. He'd said there was one particular person who had stuck in his mind by showing absolute courage and had mentioned my name.

He said: "We're out there playing a scratch match and I'm playing against this guy who's in a full burns pressure suit and he's running around like crazy going hard after the ball. Next thing you know, he's sitting on the ground undoing his boot and it's full of blood, absolutely full of blood. I asked him if he needed a hand and he just shrugged it off, laced it up and kept on training, it was absolutely unbelievable." Hearing that spurred me on even more and before long I'd decided: "Stuff it, I'm going to play."

I was preparing for my return game with Kingsley about six months after the Bali bombings and it was around this time that North Melbourne AFL player Jason McCartney, who had been injured in the bombings as well, was also working towards playing again. A week before I was due to play my first game back, I got a phone call from him.

He said: "Look, mate, I'm going to have my comeback game and I know about your story. Would you like to be a guest of ours and come down and watch? I'm inviting a fair few people who were involved to come down to a box to watch the game." I said: "Yep, no worries, I'd love to, where and when is it?" He said: "It's next week." So I postponed my own return game plans for a week. He flew me over to Melbourne and on the weekend I was supposed to have my first game back, I watched his comeback game instead. I was so inspired to get back out there myself, and the next weekend I had my shot.

I came back into Kingsley's reserves team. Running back onto the ground was unbelievable. There was a big crowd and the media came along too. I realised there was so much support out there for me. One of my friends walked around the crowd with a video camera, asking people: "What do you reckon about Phil Britten going back to play football, his first game back today?" People said things such as: "Fantastic, he's a champion; we're all here for you, Phil!" I ended up kicking four goals and felt I was flying that day.

I'd proved I could do it. I went on and played reserves all that year. My skin held up pretty well and I played most of my games in a full-length pressure suit. Towards the end of the year, I was able to wear just training tights and a full-length jumper and gloves. I used to get scratches, no different from anyone else. I suppose they just didn't heal as quickly, but the pain of the burns was now starting to fade.

That year Kingsley opened its new memorial clubrooms. The other Kingsley boys had decided, while they were on their way home from Bali, that this was the way they wanted to honour our teammates. In the immediate aftermath the Western Australian community had helped with fundraising and donations, which built us the new rooms in less than a year.

There's a memorial area set aside with photos of the boys and glass cabinets that contain some of their personal effects returned from that night, plus a lot of other items that were given to the club in support. It's like a time capsule of October 12, 2002, and I still visit there at least once a year.

There were a lot of things going on in 2003 and while it was a year of major recovery for me, I also had to begin making decisions about work and the future.

When the time came for me to try to go back to work at Direct Engineering Services, I really felt I owed it to them to be a great employee because they'd done so much for me. Because of my burns, I wasn't able to go back as a mechanic in the roof and out in the sun so instead I tried a desk job, but I just couldn't do it.

After a couple of weeks of sinking back into depression, I had to go into the boss's office and tell him. I cried in front of him and felt so ashamed that

I'd let him down. I said I really wanted to work for him but I was just a different person now and doing anything like this was making me go backwards. I said: "I'm not the same person I was and I don't think I can do this, I just have to leave."

The boss was really good to me and understood. All my colleagues supported me, understanding that I needed to go and find something else, something that would fulfil me. But I still didn't know what that was. I spent a lot of nights crying, feeling lost and without a purpose. Despite how far I'd already come, the lifestyle I loved and now the career that I'd worked so hard for had been taken away from me. I became angry once again because I felt I was always ending up back at square one.

I didn't pursue for long the offers of counselling that I was given. I did try it but I couldn't sit there with a stranger and tell them about things that they'd never truly understand. Counselling wasn't right for me. I just tried to keep it to myself and do what I thought I had to do to move past all this.

One of the hardest things for me was just going out and being part of the everyday world. I found that really, really difficult. I felt that everyone was watching me, especially in the early days, looking at my burnt and broken body and thinking: "What's wrong with that guy?"

When I had to wear the pressure suit, I felt like the boy in the bubble. In the early days, even when it was scorching hot, and I was just wearing a T-shirt and shorts, I still had on the head-to-toe suit underneath. I hated being stared at everywhere I went and I often didn't want to go out. I'd turn around, go back home, turn off all the lights, sit in a dark corner and just cry. I'd wish I was dead so that I wouldn't have to keep dealing with this.

I really feel for people who have to live with that every day of their life, those who have to live with any abnormality or deformity. People stare. I still get it to this day, even just doing everyday things. I'll go to the petrol station and when I get out to fill the tank or go up to pay I'll see their eyes. They're looking at my arms and my burns.

Some people ask: "What happened?" I let them know. I'm not ashamed of it and they usually go quiet at first, almost shocked, not believing me and then may just say something like "Oh my god..." Sometimes they're too stunned or embarrassed to say any more, but others will then have more questions, which is fine because I'm pretty open about it. Most people are good with how they handle it but others can be really hurtful, especially when they just stare for long periods of time.

There were a lot of good things going on for me, such as going back to football and getting stronger and fitter, but there were still a lot of dark times. I still had a lot of nightmares. Sometimes I'd wet the bed. I'd have a dream about going to the toilet but instead I'd wake up having already done it. I just didn't have full control back over my own body and every time it happened I felt humiliated.

The nightmares were pretty strong for about two years after Bali. I used to stress out in my sleep and the bed would just end up filled with sweat. I'd wake up and have to change the bedding every night just because of the nightmares. It was emotionally exhausting all the time.

There were all sorts of nightmares. They could be bomb-related or war-related but were always about being hurt and in pain. And there was always fire and smoke.

16

Back to Bali

THE FIRST TIME I RETURNED TO BALI WAS FOR THE TRIAL of one of the key suspects in the bombings, Amrozi. His trial started in May 2003 and he was accused of attending planning sessions for the bombings, as well as buying a tonne of explosive material and the van to be used in the biggest blast and transporting them to Bali.

He faced the death penalty under the new anti-terrorism laws that'd been enacted in Indonesia after the bombings. He'd been the first suspect arrested and was known in the media as the "smiling assassin" because of the way he was always laughing and smiling for the cameras and crowds. It was as if Amrozi thought he was a fucking celebrity.

Amrozi eventually admitted he'd bought and transported the explosives. "When I heard on the radio there were many foreign victims, I was very proud," he told the court at one stage.

The Australian government said at the time that if any of the victims were interested in going to the trial it could help us. I thought it would help me to go see it for myself.

It would also be a way for me to face some of my fears. At that stage, I was still very bitter and angry. I was angry with the people behind the bombings but hadn't really yet managed to differentiate between the bombers and the Indonesian people as a whole, including the Balinese. The idea of going back among people that I felt had tried to kill me was frightening.

Arriving in Bali stirred up really strong feelings. As soon as I landed I was hit by the intense heat and humidity. I was still in a full burns pressure suit and it felt awful, with my skin crawling and sweat pouring off my forehead. Not many people know that you don't have sweat glands on burns scars, so my only outlet to sweat and cool down is really from my head or chest. That's still how it is for me even now. I feel the heat so much more than I ever did before.

On the day of the trial, we had to make our way to the Australian Consulate in Denpasar where we'd all be taken together by bus to the court. Our group was provided with an interpreter so we'd be able to understand some of what was going on, because the whole process would be carried out in Bahasa. The court was a circus, jam-packed with onlookers and the media. I got a seat right in the centre of about the middle row.

When Amrozi walked in he had that big smile on his face and it made me burn inside with anger and hatred for him. People were yelling out "fuck you" and other stuff like that; you could feel the emotion all around, some people were shaking. It was just so intense seeing this bastard right there in front of us. There were soldiers carrying machine guns, guards and police, and he just went and sat down right in the middle of it all, seemingly oblivious to how much pain he'd caused.

The judges started talking and I found it really difficult to follow. The interpreter could only give me very brief snippets of information. They'd talk for minutes and she'd say a few words about what they were discussing. I think I ended up staying there for only 15 to 20 minutes. It was just too hard to understand and I had too much pent-up anger to sit still and listen. I felt that it was pointless for me. I thought: "I don't want to sit here any longer in the same room as this person; I'm getting out of here".

It was weird. It was one of those face-your-fear scenarios, where I wanted to see him, I wanted to see what he looked like, this monster who killed my mates and who burnt me. And yet when I got there I thought: "Oh, is that all?" The attention he was getting seemed to be feeding his ego and I wanted no part of it. Walking away was my way of saying: "You're not worth shit to me."

It was pretty disappointing that it didn't really help, that it didn't heal me in any way. I felt: "Well, this is pretty pointless. I just hate him even more now and have upset myself." And that was it. But it was something that I believed at the time that I had to do. Sometimes you walk away from things and think: "I really got a lot out of that." At other times, it doesn't work out that way. But at least I gave it a go as a way to try to deal with some of my issues.

I also saw Mira and Tansen again while I was there. My family and I had kept in touch with them and so when they found out I was going back to Bali for the trial, they arranged it so we could catch up. It was a really happy, joyous occasion seeing them again and it still felt as if they were old friends, family or godparents even.

We visited the site of the bombing together. I was overwhelmed and found it hard to reconcile that such a massacre had occurred there. I spent a lot of time in silence, as did the others. I don't think anyone really knew what to say. There weren't any words that could express what I felt. I just walked around with a huge hole in my gut that kept welling up with emotion as I looked out over the empty site.

Slowly I took it all in. I could still see tiles and parts of walls. At times, I knelt down and touched pieces of what had been the club. I don't know why, I just felt again like I was in automatic mode. Despite the bustling street and busy Kuta life going on around us, I was removed from reality, in my own world. My body was there, moving around and taking it all in, but I was actually deep inside myself, in absolute shock.

I walked over to the wall that I'd jumped over. When I got there, I touched it and thought: "I can't believe I jumped over that!" It just didn't look as if it was possible and I guess that unless you're faced with being burnt to death it might not be. I knew it was a miracle that I'd survived.

The site had a fence at the front and there were a whole pile of T-shirts hanging up that said "Fuck Terrorists". There were handwritten messages on them. There were pictures of victims, notes, banners and flags. We bought one of the "Fuck Terrorists" T-shirts, wrote a message of our own on it and hung it up with all the others.

There were many mixed emotions running through my mind, and it was just so intense that after a short while there, I was exhausted.

After visiting the site, we retraced my steps, finding exactly where I'd escaped from the club and had run down the road until Mira, Tansen and Sai rescued me.

They also took me back to the clinic where they had driven me. I met the nurses and the guy who'd driven me to the hospital. They remembered me and said: "Oh, you look different, you looked like a monster. We didn't know if you were alive or dead!"

That night we sat in the restaurant at my hotel, which overlooked the beach, and just spent time together, going over the day and, of course, connecting more dots from the night of the bombings.

In the end, being back in Bali was very helpful for me. I got to know the Balinese people. I realised I couldn't blame Bali in general for what happened to me. I came to understand that they'd been attacked as well. I learned a lot about their culture and how they felt towards the terrorists.

I was able to see what a beautiful people the Balinese are, and every time I went back that feeling grew. Now going back to Bali is easier and I'm not as self-conscious. I don't have to wear that burns pressure suit and can wear singlets and T-shirts like a normal person. People still look at me, they can see my scars, but I feel more comfortable now with myself.

And I'm stronger inside. I feel now I've got a story to tell and it doesn't matter about my burns. Local people still come up and ask what happened and when I tell them, they ask: "But why did you come back?" They're horrified that this happened to me in their country and always say: "We're so sorry." I say: "I know it wasn't Bali, Bali loves peace and it's so beautiful here." They shouldn't feel the need to apologise. I can see the pain on their faces and I know it's a pain that we share. We were all hurt deeply by what the terrorists did.

Despite coming to this understanding, it was still a bit longer until I could have the same perspective for Muslims. Mostly this was because the terrorists were Muslim and their reasoning behind the bombings was based on their religious interpretations. I was just really angry for a long time and it was easy to put them all into one category. I thought if you were a Muslim you must want to kill non-Muslims.

But again, my perspective shifted as time went on and I continued to heal. I now think that it's as simple as there are good people and there are bad people, no matter where they're from or their religion. It took me a long time to get to that point. It doesn't matter about religion or race; it's about the person. You can't put everyone with the same religion into one category. It took a long time to let go of the anger I had but it feels so much better inside to be free.

17

The first anniversary

I ALSO WENT BACK TO BALI FOR THE FIRST ANNIVERSARY of the bombings.

I knew that a lot of the guys from the footy club were thinking about going back, as were a lot of the families whose boys hadn't returned. In the end, most of those who survived went back. A few just didn't feel like they wanted or needed to.

I understood that, but I knew it would be a positive thing for me, especially because I'd missed all the funerals of my friends because I was still in hospital. I felt that going back for the anniversary service could bring me a little bit more closure. It would be a way to say my proper goodbyes, which I hadn't yet been able to do, even though I'd visited the site when I'd gone back for the trial.

This time I travelled with my extended family and Garth, one of my friends who'd really stood by me through the whole recovery process. A lot of the guys stayed at the Bounty Hotel again, but I didn't want to be near Kuta. I didn't want to be close to where the bombs had exploded. We stayed in Seminyak, outside what I saw as the danger zone, in a hotel called The Bali Mystique. I felt safer and more at peace not staying in the heart of it all.

Touching down at the airport in Denpasar was still surreal. Again, I had that sense of fear but being with my family somehow made me feel a bit safer. I felt protected. I was also still in that full burns pressure suit so, again, when I got off the plane, the heat hit me like a tonne of bricks. Even though it had been a year now since the bombings, my burns were still healing and pretty raw. They felt especially tender in the hot Bali weather.

The day before the first anniversary, there was a football match with a group of Australians who were there and we ended up drawing a large crowd. It felt really good to get the boots on, run around and release some internal pressure before facing the formalities of the next day.

On the anniversary, October 12, 2003, the Australian government and the Indonesian government had organised a massive outdoor memorial service at Garuda Wisnu Kencana Cultural Park in Jimbaran. It was a beautiful sunny day with clear blue skies and almost no wind.

We were picked up that morning and taken in a bus to the service with the other Kingsley guys. We drove for ages to get there, up through the hills, and it felt very removed from where the bombs exploded the year before, but in a good way.

Before we left Australia, we'd been given blue and gold brooches by the government to help identify those who'd been directly involved. This was to stop us being checked at every point under very tight security, and it meant we could pay our respects in peace.

The park was a beautiful place and the service was held in an area that was almost like a large quarry. We had to walk for quite some time to get there. We went along walkways, up stairs, down stairs and finally arrived at an enclosed area with massive steps built into the walls. On the way in, pictures of those who had lost their lives lined the walls. It was all stone, almost like marble, and there were big statues. Everyone was silent; there was so much emotion in the air. The speakers stood at the front of the crowd on a podium. There was seating available as well as room for people to stand towards the back. I was seated in a VIP area with the other guys from Kingsley footy club and my family.

There were thousands of people there. The name of every single person who had died was read out. When they read out the names of all our mates, everyone around us was crying. I've never cried so much in my life, and once we got out all those tears, all that hurt, it was a huge relief for me.

It was another big release of pent-up emotions. I guess many of us had tried to be as strong as we could through the year after the bombing and had tried not to show our feelings. But here, we could finally let go.

It wasn't just tough for the guys who were badly injured. It was also tough for the guys who hadn't been so badly hurt. They'd experienced a hell of a lot as well. So that service was also a huge weight off their shoulders. We all walked around afterwards, hugging each other. It was a crazy, crazy day.

The Australian prime minister at the time, John Howard, was there and I met him after the service. He shook people's hands as they left, thanking as many as he could for coming.

Later in the afternoon, I went down to the beach in Kuta where there was a massive surfboard ceremony, Paddle for Peace. People on more than 50 surfboards carried dozens of wreaths into the ocean and, as it got closer to sunset, candles were lit along the beach in remembrance.

Mr Howard was there again, with a crowd of thousands, including a lot of Australians. Everyone was revved up in a good way and we all marched down the beach together. At some point, I was given a megaphone and belted out a couple of "Aussie, Aussie, Aussie, Oi, Oi, Oi" chants. The atmosphere was electric – a rousing act of defiance against terrorists. It was as if we were showing them that they would not succeed, that we were united. There was no hate, no fear, just a lot of powerful strength coming from all of us.

After the march, the crowd gathered and there was a microphone available where people could go and say something, anything, really, that was on their mind. I decided to get up and say exactly how I felt inside. I said: "They can try to hurt us, they can take away our loved ones and try to make us afraid, but they can't take away our spirit! We're here and together we'll overcome!"

After that, we went back to a hotel in Kuta where one of the footy guys was staying. We all lounged around, swam and had a few beers. Now that the official goodbye was over, we ended up getting a bit drunk. It was a relief that it was done, like a wake after attending someone's funeral. We spent time celebrating life and the fact that we were alive, while also shedding a few more tears for those we didn't have with us on this trip.

That night we decided to go back to the places we'd been the year before. Our group included some of the fathers who had lost sons in the bombing. We went first to Bagus Bar to have a meal and a few beers.

It was a strange feeling knowing that this was the last place that we really saw all our mates together. There were lots more tears, and from one moment to the next you could be either laughing or crying.

In some ways, it was almost like the year before but, of course, this time there was a different feeling to it all. This time, instead of being on top of the world, we'd been to hell and back.

The staff knew Kevin Paltridge (father of Corey Paltridge who'd died in 2002) and a few of the other guys who had already been there during the past year, but I didn't really talk with them about any of it. It felt good in a way to take the dads back to the last place where their boys had been so happy. Perhaps it also helped them piece together more of that night, and hopefully added to their memories of their sons.

There were a few times when I looked around and it crossed my mind that it could happen again that night. I wasn't nervous. It was just surreal.

About 10.30 pm, we walked around the corner to where the Sari Club had been. Security was tight and police had blocked off the road so that people couldn't drive past. They were worried about another attack. I did get nervous at that point, but I put it out of my mind. We were on a mission.

The banners and other items that had been put up over the past year were still there, with some fresh tributes. Photos and flowers lined the fence. We were still able to walk onto the site, and there was still some of the flooring and other remnants around.

It was a weird feeling to be back on the site, as if we were in a graveyard full of the souls of those we'd lost. It was a place where we felt the need to be quiet and respectful. I don't recall having any particular thoughts at that point. I just stood there, still, trying to feel and connect with where I was, and to take in what had happened exactly a year earlier. There was so much pain in the crowd. Candles had been lit and it seemed that thousands of people had gathered and were all standing together as one.

At 11.08 pm, the time the bomb had gone off exactly one year before, there was silence. Many just stood there, sobbing and holding hands.

I also walked over the road to visit the memorial. We stayed around the site and memorial for about another 20 minutes. There were hugs and tears. Once it was over, I finally went back to my hotel.

I think the rest of the guys went out and had a few more drinks that night but I just wasn't ready for that yet. It took a long, long time for me to be able to go out to a club, have a drink and be around music, even back at home, because it just reminded me too much of the bombings. To go back into the same kind of environment at that time was really scary for me. I just couldn't do it.

I've been back to Bali a few other times since and it still gives me mixed feelings. Recently, we drove through Kuta, along Jalan Legian, past the bombing site at night, and the place was pumping. I looked around and although I wasn't fearful, I felt as if I'd stepped back in time and was watching a movie of the night the bombs went off. There was music, lights and people walking around, laughing and having a good time. I thought to myself: "Wow, it could happen. It could still happen and these guys and girls wouldn't have a clue, just like I didn't."

You can't live your life in fear and now I could walk into one of those places and have a beer or a meal and walk out again, but it's just not something I want to do. It just brings back memories I don't need to re-live any more.

18

Opening up

GRADUALLY, I STARTED TO TALK MORE OPENLY ABOUT what I'd gone through.

It seemed to come out of my questioning of what I was going to do with my life. I just thought: "Well, right now, I'm not doing anything." People started asking me questions and I just began answering them.

I told them the whole story and they were amazed at how much I remembered. And after hearing what I'd gone through, they were also amazed that I'd survived. I would often get very upset while I spoke, but afterwards, even if I'd spoken to a random stranger, I felt a sort of relief.

Somehow, talking about things seemed to be working for me. I was unburdening myself of all this heaviness that I had been carrying around. My Grandma Clare then suggested that perhaps I could help others along the way.

She asked whom I'd most like to help, and I looked back and thought of the battered old ambulance that the clinic in Kuta had put me in to take me to the hospital. I realised that old van had played a big part in my still being here.

I thought: "What if they hadn't had the van, and what if the van hadn't worked?" I really felt it would be good to help the clinic to raise funds for a new ambulance. We worked out we would need about $50,000, and it seemed that, with all the support I was getting from the community, it was achievable.

My Grandma Clare knew that the local Lions clubs of Perth raised and donated money to worthy causes, and so I began to get involved in public speaking. I did a talk for a local Lions club and even though it was only a small affair of maybe 50 people, it was absolutely nerve-wracking.

I wasn't the type of person who naturally wanted to talk in front of a crowd. It's a skill, and some lucky people are born with it. I was only good at leading a football team, not so good at standing in front of a crowd of people, telling them about my life.

But I had a go. I stood up and just recounted what had happened from the time we got to the airport all the way through to when I went back to playing football. During the speech, people started to cry. I got choked up with emotion too. My voice quivered a lot, not from nerves but because it still hurt so much inside. I still get the same way, even now, when I think or talk about my friends, my mates who died and those who I've still got.

My first talk went for 90 minutes. I cried almost the whole way through. At the end, I got a standing ovation. I just wasn't prepared for it, and what happened next was the reason I kept doing it. Almost every person in the room came up to me and said: "Wow, that was just so inspiring and I wish that my grandson or granddaughter could be a quarter as determined as you are. What an amazing story." They had tears in their eyes and I realised I'd moved something inside them.

It went on from there. I was asked to speak to other groups, and in a way the talks were like my own counselling sessions. I walked away each time feeling lighter instead of heavier. I'd tell my story and I'd cry quite a bit, then people would tell me how amazing I was just for being me, for getting through what had happened, and that I was doing a great job.

I think it was at this point that I started to turn a corner in my recovery. It was ironic in a way. I was in this really dark place, yet everyone was looking at me and seeing someone inspirational instead of looking at me and seeing just my physical deformities and feeling sorry for me. I'd been feeling really down, but at these talks people saw me completely differently from how I saw myself, and it helped give me a new perspective.

The turnaround was very gradual though. For me it didn't matter how much I inspired people, there was still a lot of hurt, doubt and darkness inside me. The recovery didn't happen overnight, it didn't happen over a year. It just happened slowly over time and I guess it's still happening.

I must have spoken at most of the Lions clubs in WA, even some out in the Wheatbelt and up north.

Some of the events were really big, with a few hundred or more people. I went to Darwin in April 2004 and spoke at the National Safety Council to a miners' safety group. While I was there, I also got the chance to visit Darwin Hospital where I'd been stabilised on my way to Adelaide.

I was able to thank the staff who'd helped save my life and talk to them about the sense of relief I'd felt when I'd arrived in Australia and how I'd just let go, ready to die when I got home, placing my destiny in their hands.

No matter how many times I did these talks, or the size of the crowd, I still found preparing to go out in front of audiences terrifying.

But what eased the pressure was that I was talking about the truth, about myself and something that I'd done. No talk was ever the same as another because it was never scripted or staged – no dot points or palm cards. I just got up and talked, opening up more and more each time.

At the end of each session, there was time for a few questions. People would ask me how I felt about the people who had done this to me, about whether I'd changed. I'd simply say: "Well, this is how I feel today. Yes, I hate them with a passion. They killed seven of my friends, 88 Australians, 202 people. They burnt half of my body, bashed out my teeth. So yeah, I hate them."

I suppose I still hate them and what they did, but I have also learnt to not let it consume me any more. Hate takes up so much energy and when I decided to stop giving them my time, like when I walked out of Amrozi's trial, I realised that this was how I could be free again. It was how I could stop feeling like a victim and start feeling like a survivor instead.

Anyone who's put in a situation like mine no doubt goes through a similar change. They'll process it the best way they know how and deal with it the best way they can. It's a journey that takes time.

Just from doing the talks at Lions clubs, I raised about $10,000. We investigated further how much it would cost not just to buy an ambulance for the clinic in Bali but what we'd need to do to get it there and have it set up. Soon, we realised how much red tape there was to get through.

It's not as simple as buying someone an ambulance. We'd have to ship it over there and pay for freight costs. It'd have to be licensed in Indonesia and it was going to end up costing more money than we'd anticipated, and definitely more than I could raise by myself. We decided instead to donate the $10,000 to Dr Fiona Wood's McComb Foundation for Burns Research, which was the other cause close to my heart.

I was also still struggling at this time with what to do about work in the long term. Towards the end of 2003, I'd decided to try a new path. I went to a technical and further education college (TAFE) and did a certificate in occupational health and safety. I thought that perhaps I could use my experiences to help people prevent hazardous events in the workplace. I thought I might have something to give in that area.

I went to TAFE for six months, part-time three or four days a week, and I started instructing in martial arts on a casual basis.

Returning to martial arts came about after I'd spoken to my old instructor. I said to him: "I just want to get back into martial arts. I don't know if I can or I can't, but I'm back playing football and so I'd like to give it a shot." And so, just like football, it started with one training session a week, in a full burns pressure suit, then two or three sessions, and it just grew from there.

I was just trying it to see whether I could do it, and in 2003, in my first year back to Zen Do Kai, I was awarded WA State black belt of the year. There was no thought at that time that it would lead to me becoming a martial arts instructor, let alone a business owner. Once I got into it again, my instructor said: "Well, have you ever thought about maybe helping to teach in class?" I said: "No, not really." But then one of the instructors went on holidays and I was asked to help while he was away.

The next thing I knew, he decided not to come back and so I ended up taking over his position permanently.

I'd finish TAFE at 2.30 pm and go straight to work at the martial arts centre. There was a little overlap there for a time, but in 2004, I thought, well, I know I can get a full-time job as a martial arts instructor. I liked it and I was good at it, so when I'd finished my diploma, I put my thoughts of occupational health and safety to rest and instead started teaching martial arts as a career.

It was strange how it worked out. I just found the path that I was meant to take. When I was on the right track, I felt fulfilled and my motivation grew and grew.

19

Falling in love

SOMETHING ELSE POSITIVE WAS HAPPENING IN MY LIFE, which would also become a huge turning point for me. I'd started to fall in love.

I first met Rebecca in 2003 through the Kingsley Football Club. I'd met her on the sidelines the year after Bali when her boyfriend had started to play with us and she often came down to watch the games.

We also ended up having some mutual friends, so I'd see her out at parties. Even though we spoke occasionally, we never really got to know each other very well that first year.

Even in the early days, I was attracted to her and enjoyed being around her but that was about it — we were both dating other people. It wasn't until late 2004 that we realised we both had feelings for each other and actually spoke about it.

The only trouble was that I realised she felt the same way I did on the night before she left for Europe. We left it at that but I couldn't get her out of my mind. I felt that I wanted to see her again.

But by that time, she was already on her way to the other side of the world. Even though we knew each other socially, I didn't know much else about her – not even her surname.

So I decided to wait to see whether she came back. And six months later, out of the blue, I bumped into her at the Kingsley Tavern. She was meeting some friends for a drink and I ended up joining her for a while. It wasn't until she was leaving that I decided to say something to her and give her my number.

We ended up catching up the next day and again the following weekend and I was really happy but then I just freaked out, I don't know why. I didn't answer her calls or texts and so she stopped trying to reach me.

I knew I was going to fall in love and wasn't really ready for it yet. I was still suffering some depression, just starting to figure out who I was and what I wanted out of life.

It was about that time that I started going out again more, hitting the clubs and partying hard. It had taken a long time for me to be able to relax and have a drink again. I wasn't going to be afraid of being targeted by terrorists just for being young and wanting a good time.

As well as going out partying, I threw myself back into playing football with Kingsley and was working full-time as a martial arts instructor and occasionally as security in local pubs. It felt like I was always busy and even though I was still battling the depression inside, I didn't really have time to think about it.

It was also around this stage that I went out and got my first tattoo. The guys from Kingsley who'd come back from Bali had all got memorial tattoos not long after the bombings but I couldn't because of my scars. So, in 2005, my skin had healed well enough and I'd heard that it would actually help flatten out some of the scar tissue so I decided to get my own version. I had quite a large tattoo done on my torso, from my ribcage to my waist.

On it were the names of all the boys from the club who had died in the attacks, and the words "Sari Club,

Kuta Bali, 2002". The design included fire and a tiger leaping from the flames. Our club was the "Kingsley Cats" and when it was drawn for me, it just felt right.

I still thought about Rebecca often and would get in touch with her from time to time. I knew how she felt about me and I felt the same but I just wasn't ready. I know she was hurt about that but instead of being angry and walking away, she told me to figure it all out, that if it was meant to be, we'd eventually end up together. I believed that too, which is probably what helped see us through the tough times.

We saw each other on and off for most of 2005 but halfway through the year I decided I needed to see more of the world and go travelling. Deep down, I also didn't know whether I wanted to come back to Perth. I hadn't figured out yet where I wanted my life to end up. It was going to be a completely open-ended trip and the prospect of that was exciting!

I had to tell Rebecca that I was leaving Perth and I wasn't sure that I'd be coming back. We just tried to stay light-hearted about it all. It was hard walking away but this was something I had to do for me.

In September 2005, I set off with Brad McIlroy, who'd been in Bali with me. We met other friends along the way and travelled Europe for two months and America for two months.

It was something I'd long promised myself and an amazing eye-opener. It felt great that I'd finally seen more of the world.

20

Bali targeted again

IN ON OCTOBER 1, 2005, JUST AS WE WERE ALL STARTING to get our lives back on track, terrorist bombers hit Bali again. This time they killed 20 people, four of them Australians.

I was still on my big overseas trip at the time and was in London. Since 2002 I'd been getting regular calls from the media about Bali. Whenever there was anything that happened that could be linked in some way to a terrorist attack, journalists would find me.

They'd always ask me the same question: "How do you feel about it?" I'd got sick of talking about it and stopped taking calls from anyone in the media. I just didn't answer numbers that I didn't know any more.

But when my mobile phone rang this time, I thought it was one of my friends, so I answered, and it was a journalist.

I can't remember who it was or which organisation they were from. They said: "Hi Phil, it's so and so from somewhere, I just wanted to know if I can have a quick word with you." I'd had a few drinks at that stage and I still didn't really know who it was.

They told me there had been another bombing in Bali and wanted to know my thoughts. I just remember saying something like: "Sorry, this is the first I've heard of it and I don't really have any thoughts at the moment."

I was a bit angry that they'd called me, and when I hung up it was a strange feeling. I was in a bar, the exact type of place I'd been in when it happened to me in 2002. I couldn't help but think about it. I just hoped that this time no one I knew had been hurt.

I really felt for those who were caught up in it, those who would be frantically trying to find their families who were in Bali, those who were injured and in pain, and those whose lives had just been lost in such a horrible way.

But it also brought me back to my past, the very thing I was trying to get away from by travelling.

I was in another country. No one knew who I was and if someone saw my burns, it wouldn't matter; no one would know where they'd come from.

In Europe I wasn't a Bali bomb survivor, I was just Phil from Australia. The essence of that trip was to be someone that I'd never been before and maybe someone I could have been if I hadn't been in Bali.

On the third anniversary of the Sari Club bombing, October 12, 2005, I was in Edinburgh with Brad McIlroy and Kal Zomer (who was also in Bali with us in 2002).

We were all in a pretty rebellious and self-destructive stage at that time in our lives. It was almost like I was challenging life to see what it could throw at me to prove that I could take it. Fortunately, I moved through it, because it took its toll. It was all part of the recovery process. I'd gone through anger, depression, resignation, and now I was facing things head-on and pushing myself past every limit that I could find.

So there we were, three years on from the bombings, sitting in a bar, thinking about the friends we'd lost. We had a drinking ritual. We each had one shot of Sambuca for every friend we'd lost and it was always messy. We were celebrating their lives and our lives, but also we were mourning the loss and it ended in tears and hugging each other. It still ends like that every year.

There's a memorial in Kings Park, Western Australia, which was established in 2003. This is where most of us gather now at dawn on the anniversary. We often have a barbecue somewhere afterwards with the guys from Kingsley, play some cricket and try to have a few laughs. It's a time where we can catch up with old friends we haven't seen for a while and also support each other through what still is a really hard day to deal with.

21

Ready to move on

WHEN I GOT BACK FROM EUROPE IN LATE 2005, I WAS finally clear about exactly where I was going. The trip had been a time of soul-searching. I'd thought about Rebecca a lot but had decided not to keep in touch with her while I was away. I hadn't told her when I was coming back and she hadn't asked. Being in Europe, I'd wanted to be by myself, to be free and see the world. And it had cleared my head so that I could see that what I really wanted was to be with Rebecca.

Towards the end of the trip, I'd made a decision and knew that when I got back to Perth, I wanted to settle down with her and start a proper relationship. Because we hadn't kept in touch, I wasn't even 100 per cent sure that she was still living in Perth. She'd talked a lot about moving interstate and travelling.

I'd also made up my mind about my work direction. I knew that one day I wanted to start my own martial arts school, not just to teach but also to have my very own school. And to test myself, I decided that one day I wanted to step into the ring and have a full contact Muay Thai kickboxing fight.

The day I got home, I called my friends and we organised to go out for a drink. Rebecca was there that night but she left early. It wasn't until a few days later, on Christmas Eve, that I had a party at my house with a few friends and we got a chance to speak.

I told her I was in love with her, and luckily, she was still in love with me too. We spent a lot of time together after that and it felt so natural this time, we just slipped straight into a relationship.

About six months later she surprised me with a trip to Brunei for my birthday. When I arrived and unpacked, I realised that I'd left my long-sleeve protective vest behind. I still never went out in public with my burns showing and freaked out a little.

I lied and told her that I needed my vest to cover up from the sun but she just shrugged and said: "It's OK, I burn easily so we'll stay in the shade," and before I knew it, I was walking around in just a pair of board shorts on my way to the pool. That was the last time I worried about covering up my scars.

We spent a lot of time with the locals, who were Muslim, and that trip also helped heal me a lot more. In Brunei, it doesn't matter if you are Muslim, Christian or whatever: everyone appreciates you for who you are instead of what you are. I came home from Brunei feeling lighter inside, like I'd somehow let go of even more self-doubt and pain.

And it was there that I asked Rebecca to move in with me when we got back to Perth.

We often talked about our dreams and aspirations. One night, I told Rebecca that eventually I wanted to own a martial arts school, and she surprised me by saying: "Go for it, but why one day? Why not now?" We lived together, she said she'd be there to support me and we'd just make it work somehow. I started working on a business plan the very next day.

By 2007, we'd been together for a year and a half and I opened up my first martial arts school with a business partner.

It grew pretty quickly to a membership of 100 students, which was unbelievable. And then, around the same time as we opened the business, I decided to take on the full contact Muay Thai fight. I was really close to the event when the legacy of the bombings came back again. I'd always had aches and pains since 2002, but had recently developed a pain through my right leg. I thought I'd just injured my knee and rested, but it didn't go away. Rebecca made me see a doctor and that's when I found out that it wasn't a knee injury. The pain was coming from my spine.

When I was hit by the blast in 2002, I'd been thrown backwards, hyper-extending my back, and my vertebrae had shifted. Over time, it had put pressure on the disc and now it was bulging out, pinching on a nerve. The pain went down into my right knee.

The doctor sent me to a specialist a week before the fight. The specialist said, "Well, the pain's there, you can't really do any more damage, it's a nerve pain. If you can put up with the pain, you'll be fine. Think about it, only you know your body, but we'll need to operate at some stage."

The fight meant so much to me and with over 100 people coming to support me, I decided to go ahead. I was just going to use my left leg and try to keep my weight off my right side.

That week, I fought in the ring and won. It felt amazing. I had a whole group of supporters there cheering me on, and after the trophies were presented, all the boys from Kingsley, wearing their footy jumpers, and Rebecca, who was wearing my number 4 jumper, were allowed into the ring and jumped up to congratulate me. Everyone knew how much it meant, that it wasn't just a win in the kickboxing ring. It was a win against my injuries and the demons I'd battled inside and had overcome.

After the fight, I tried to put the pain out of my mind. I couldn't bear the thought of another operation. I felt all right for a while, but sure enough, it came back and at times it would get to the point where I couldn't walk properly and even coughing or sneezing would hurt.

This was also the end of football for me. I always played hard out on the field and had reached the level I'd been at before Bali, or maybe even better. By now, I'd done more than reach my initial goal of just returning to football; I'd ended up playing with the league side for almost another five years. It was time to stop.

On top of what was happening physically, I also had a choice to make about my extra commitments.

You can't train for football properly and run a martial arts school. In my last year of football, I didn't train because I was working so hard on building the business, so I just played on the weekends. That ruffled a few feathers at the club because they had a policy that if you can't train, you don't play. But the coach and I both knew how committed I was and that I trained by myself all week in martial arts. He knew I was fit and good and so made me an exception. But I still felt bad about it, so the decision to stop playing was also, in a way, a relief.

I planned to have my spinal operation in mid 2008 but first I had a family holiday planned and had decided to propose to Rebecca.

22

Two steps forward, one back

I'D ALWAYS SEEN MYSELF GETTING MARRIED AND starting a family, and now I knew this was what I wanted with Rebecca. It was really just a matter of timing. The right marriage proposal was important to me and it had to be something special.

Rebecca's family had often been to Bali for holidays, but since we'd been together, she hadn't gone back because she knew how I felt. She did ask me once if I ever wanted to go back, and I told her flat out that no, it wasn't something I wanted to do, that I just didn't see it as a holiday destination where I could relax.

But in September 2007 Rebecca's step-mum Helene won some money playing Lotto and was going to pay for us to join them on a holiday. Immediately, everyone started talking about going to Bali, but then they remembered that I wasn't keen, and offered to go somewhere else.

But I knew how much Bali meant to Rebecca's family. I thought about it for a while and decided it would be the perfect place for me to propose. We'd be at her childhood holiday destination with her extended family, including grandparents, aunts, uncles and cousins. And it would mark a new beginning for both of us.

The holiday was booked for April 2008 and I went out and put a deposit on the ring that I'd chosen. I also decided to videotape each stage leading up to the proposal so Rebecca could watch it afterwards and see what I'd been up to.

I taped myself bringing the ring home, hiding it in my gym gear and the days leading up to the holiday, kind of like a video diary. I also videotaped myself going to ask her father's permission. About a week before we left, I called her dad, Henry, while he was at work and said: "I need to come and have a chat with you." He thought that I was going to say that I couldn't go to Bali because of the issues that I had, so asking instead to marry his daughter was a bit unexpected. Luckily, he was just as excited as I was and said he'd be happy to help with the surprise.

Maybe it was because I was going to be with Rebecca's family on holiday, in an area outside Kuta, that I felt safer this time. It was almost as if I wasn't even in Bali. I proposed the first night, at dinner on the beach with her dad's family all there.

People often ask me: "Why would you do that in Bali after all you went through there?" I say: "Well, it was more about family and memories, and Bali is somewhere that has always been so special to Rebecca. I wanted to be a part of that." It was good for me. When I think of Bali, I still do think of the terrorist attack but I can also see what made Bali so special for Rebecca and her family. Now I'm a part of the memories they've created there and I've created some happy memories of my own.

We even considered getting married in Bali. We looked into it while we were there and spoke to a few people, but realised if we did it overseas, not everyone we wanted there would be able to make it. So we decided to get married back home in Perth and set the date for February 28, 2009.

Before that though, I still had to get my spinal operation out of the way. I just wanted to get it over with. It was terrifying as it'd been a while since I'd been in hospital and I ended up feeling a bit depressed about it all. I also needed to take a lot of extra precautions because of the risk of infection in my burns scars.

I did end up getting an infection, but we got to it in time and there were no serious complications. Everything else went really well with the operation and I went back to work after a few weeks off.

It was also around this time that the Bali bombing saga was once again playing out in the media as the bombers were set to be executed. It seemed that every day there was a news story about it and we were constantly getting phone calls from journalists. The bombers' faces were on the TV and in newspapers almost daily. It made me sick to see their smiling faces and it was really hard to switch off from it all.

What made it worse was that it was mostly specu-lation about what was going to happen or about them launching another appeal against their executions. I didn't give a crap what was going to happen to them. I just hoped that it would all be over soon and they'd stop swanning about like movie stars; they were mass murderers!

Rebecca and I decided to call the Australian Federal Police (AFP) to find out more about what was going on. After we explained who we were, they assured us that if anything happened, they would let us know directly and we could simply ignore all the media hype.

Whether we were for or against the death penalty was completely irrelevant; having it played out day after day, week after week, was something that no one who'd suffered from the bombers' actions needed to keep going through.

Finally, one morning at about 4 am, our phones started ringing. The news was filtering through that the bombers had been executed overnight in Indonesia. I spoke with the AFP on our home phone while Rebecca spoke to one of our friends on my mobile. The fact that the AFP had kept their word and let us know almost immediately after the event meant a lot to me. They really went above and beyond to make sure that those who were directly affected by the bombings were personally updated where possible. One rumour I did hear afterwards was that when faced with the firing squad, Amrozi finally stopped smiling.

When we hung up, we had a strange feeling. Did we celebrate that it was finally over? We really didn't know what to do, we just looked at each other in the dark and said, "Well, that's it then, it's done." It felt odd, like I was stunned or numb. After that, we just rolled over to go back to sleep but it wasn't long until the media hype began again.

We arranged to go to the Kingsley Tavern to meet some of the Kingsley boys – most people who I'd been in Bali with had decided to take the day off work as the news spread. When we arrived there were journalists and cameras everywhere. If we hugged someone to say "Hello" cameras snapped away. The media were all just standing around in a group, not really knowing how to approach us. I know that it was a story they needed to cover and I'm sure it was uncomfortable for them as they tried to do their job without intruding.

We agreed to do an interview and allow some photos to be taken after we'd visited some of the Kingsley boys' graves to pay our respects. It was such a strange day – some people celebrated, some people quietly reflected – but overall, we knew it meant another step towards closure.

What I've found about closure is that the saying "When one door closes, another one opens" is so true. While all this was being played out, Rebecca and I were being presented with a new business venture that we were really excited about.

The martial arts school that I'd trained at and worked in before opening my own was up for sale and we'd been approached to take it over in a partnership with Graham McDonnell, a guy I'd trained alongside for years. Graham and I knew it would be a successful partnership because we'd worked together as senior instructors and just bounced off each other with our energy.

About to get married and hoping to start a family, we were both in the same position, and decided to go for it. I sold my share of our other martial arts business back to my then business partner, re-mortgaged our house and jumped head first into developing what is now known as *The WA Institute of Martial Arts (WAIMA)* and *Predator Muay Thai*.

It was one of the best decisions we've ever made. The business has expanded beyond our wildest dreams, and in partnership with Graham and his wife Deanne, we're working hard every day to develop new ventures.

However, as has been the case with my life since 2002, I often found myself on a bit of a rollercoaster ride. Just as we got stuck into getting WAIMA off the ground in late 2008, I was crippled once again with back pain and had to return to see my specialist. He did some tests and it turned out that the operation I'd had, which had simply shaved off the bulging bit of my disc, wasn't enough. I now needed a spinal fusion to prop up the area that was being pinched.

Unfortunately, not only were we starting a new business venture together, it was now really close to our wedding. We knew that the recovery could take some time but if I didn't get it done, I'd barely be able to stand up for the ceremony, let alone go away on a honeymoon. We decided that I needed the surgery and if need be would postpone the wedding. Graham also supported me in this decision and encouraged me to get it sorted out as soon as possible.

The recovery was a bit longer this time but there was no infection, which helped. I came out of hospital on Christmas Eve 2008, only eight weeks or so before our wedding day. The nerve pain had gone and as I healed from the operation, combined with ongoing weekly chiropractic care, I was finally pain-free again and ready for the big day.

We were married in Fremantle, Western Australia, at a beautiful old church and held our reception on a yacht. It was perfect. Mira and Tansen also surprised me at the church. We'd invited them, and I knew they were hoping to make it but I wasn't 100 per cent sure that they were definitely coming until I saw them on the day.

We had our honeymoon in Phuket, Thailand, and had decided not to wait to start a family. Just after we got back from the honeymoon, we found out we were pregnant, and in January 2010 Rebecca gave birth to our son, Benjamin Philip. Our second son, Riley James, was born in April 2012. It was love at first sight for both of us.

Becoming a dad has changed me in so many ways. It's brought Rebecca and I even closer together and made me stop and appreciate more of the little things in life. I want, even more than ever now, to be a positive role model for my children and show them that no matter what happens to you outside of your control, you still ultimately choose what path you take.

It also gave me a deeper appreciation of what my parents must have gone through while I was missing in Bali and then while I was struggling with my recovery. It's a hard thing to understand until you become a parent yourself.

23

Stepping up for peace

ANOTHER POSITIVE ASPECT OF MY LIFE HAS BEEN MY involvement in the Bali Peace Park project. The idea of creating a spiritual garden and museum at the site of the Sari Club led to the formation of the Bali Peace Park Association Inc. in 2008. The association's board is made up of survivors of the 2002 and 2005 terrorist attacks, their relatives, friends and supporters.

It's a non–profit organisation based on developing the site into a green space where people can sit and reflect. It's unique in that it is designed to have four "contemplation" corners for followers of four religions: Hindus, Muslims, Buddhists and Christians, all together in one space.

Nick Way, a journalist from Perth who'd covered the Bali bombings in 2002 and 2005, was the key to Rebecca and I getting involved in the project. He and I had met a number of times over the years. He had been one of the first journalists on the scene, had seen a lot himself, and felt the need as much as we did to do something positive with the site.

He telephoned one day and said: "Look, Phil, I'd like to come over. I've got this project that I'm thinking about working on and I've got Gary Nash and a few others who survived Bali helping out as well. I just want to know if you're interested in having a chat."

So he came over and we talked about the idea. It had been raised in the past but hadn't really gone far. He proposed that a group of us take it on with a fresh perspective and give it another go. The people who'd worked on it in the past also endorsed us to see whether we could make it happen.

I wanted to know what Rebecca thought and whether she'd be involved too. She was keen, so we had another meeting with Nick and Karen Way, Gary Nash, his wife, Sharon, and Kevin Paltridge, whose son Corey died in 2002. We just thought: "Do we want to see cars parked on the Sari Club site as it is now, or do we want to push for a garden-style peace park on the land? Let's give it a go!"

Rebecca took on the role of secretary and I became a spokesperson. Working on the project has brought the group together like a close-knit family. We've all been through something life-changing with the events in Bali and we understand each other.

First we sat down and put together a plan. A lot of what we would need to do was new to us. We formed an advisory panel to help us navigate around some of the obstacles that were put in our way. There was also some commercial interest in the property, which emerged not long after we'd started working on the Peace Park.

One idea, which we came up against, was a plan to develop another bar on the site, but the concept upset a lot of people. Thankfully, the Balinese government was adamant that it would only endorse a Peace Park development, and believed in it as much as we did.

I've had to go to Bali a few times for meetings but have only had to stay a day or two, depending on how much work we have to get done while we're there. There have been some surreal moments, such as holding press conferences at the site and meetings with dignitaries, including the Bali Governor Made

Mangku Pastika. One of the times I had to go for a site visit was only a week and a half before our son Benjamin was due. I stood there and thought: "Wow, my life has changed so much since the bombings," and got a bit choked up thinking about it all.

At the moment, we're in the final stages of the project. We've got a significant amount of funding pledged and are hoping to open in time for the 10th anniversary of the bombing in 2012.

To be able to visit the Peace Park with all my friends and family 10 years after the bombing and know I was a part of its creation will be an incredible feeling.

24

A wife's perspective – Rebecca Britten

SUNDAY, OCTOBER 13, 2002 I WAS WOKEN BY THE home telephone ringing incessantly. I sat up, noticed it was barely even dawn and remembered my parents had left to begin their holiday in Europe overnight.

I leapt up and flew down the hall, wondering what on earth was going on, hoping that nothing serious had happened.

When I answered the phone, I heard my mum's voice. She told me that there'd been a terrorist attack in Bali and the airport was chaos. She assured me that everything was still OK and they would soon be leaving as planned.

I turned on the TV to watch the news unfold. We'd holidayed almost annually in Bali since I was a small child and had family who lived there. I watched the scenes on TV in utter disbelief as the idyllic island images I'd grown up with were replaced by scenes of carnage and mayhem.

The news began to filter through that a local group of boys from the Kingsley Football Club had been caught up in the bombing and a lot of them were missing. I'd grown up in Woodvale, which was the suburb next to Kingsley. I knew then that this was going to affect my local community in a big way.

Suddenly, I remembered that I'd recently seen that exact group of guys at a local bar.

They'd just won their grand final and were pretty rowdy, so it was impossible not to notice them. They were the type of group that you'd look over towards and laugh or smile at, because they were having so much fun. I remember the DJ giving them a shout-out and the boys responding with a loud cheer as they held their medals up high, enjoying their victory.

I couldn't help but wonder as I sat there, a little over a week after that night at the bar, how many of them were now missing, or dead? The words just kept going through my head: "What...? How...?"

A week later, a candle-lit vigil was held at the Kingsley Football Club oval to support the families of those affected. I went along with my friends and joined a 10,000-strong crowd. It was an awe-inspiring sight and something that brought everyone I saw to tears. I remember that as songs were being sung, an older woman I'd never met turned to me and gave me a hug. I hugged her back and we linked arms for a while. That's how it was that night; there were no strangers, everyone was there to support each other.

After that, prayers were said, words of support and encouragement offered up into the night for one of the players who was in Royal Adelaide Hospital, fighting for his life.

I had no idea that the guy I was saying a silent prayer for was going to be my husband and the father of my children.

The community support for the footy club continued into the 2003 season. A guy I was dating at the time decided to sign up to play with Kingsley along with some of his friends, and in autumn that year I was back on the footy oval, but this time I was on the sidelines, cheering on the team.

I don't remember the exact moment Phil and I met. I do, however, remember his first game back for Kingsley. It was a moment of pride for everyone there. Even if you'd never met him, you admired the obvious strength and courage he'd displayed by getting back out there so soon after the bombing. I cheered him on along with the rest of the crowd.

Our first real conversation was about his fund-raising for an ambulance. And it was the first time I realised the effect he had on me. Instead of being able to say what I wanted to, I just remember blushing and mumbling something about a few ideas I had that might help. He smiled, said "Thanks" and I walked away feeling like an absolute idiot.

A few weeks later, Phil appeared on the TV while I was helping my mum in the kitchen. It took me a few seconds to realise that I'd stopped chopping vegetables to listen to him speak. My mum took one look at me, laughed and said: "You like that guy!" to which I quickly backtracked and told her that she definitely had it all wrong.

But I knew deep down she was right.

Eventually, one night, when I was out and had enjoyed a few too many drinks, I blurted out to him what my mum had said to me, expecting us both to laugh about it. But instead Phil stopped and seemed to look at me seriously, then smiled and said: "What?" I laughed it off and we chatted a while longer.

Not long after, he leaned in and kissed me. I think we both shocked ourselves and didn't really know what to say. Then we began to talk and for the first time had a long conversation about a lot of things going on in our lives. We realised we had a lot in common, and when he left that night I knew that something important in my life had just happened.

It was almost six months before I saw Phil again. I'd left for Europe the day after our kiss and needed to figure out some things. I was in a relationship that had become increasingly volatile over the past year and I was afraid that Phil was just my way of trying to escape reality. Even worse, I was afraid that if he wasn't, I'd have ruined any chance we'd had by starting it the wrong way.

Eventually we bumped into each other again and after a few hours of awkward small talk, we both admitted that not much had changed in how we felt. And we were now both single.

There was a lot of baggage still around for both of us though, so while we dated casually on and off for a while, it wasn't until almost a year and half after our first kiss that we finally decided to start a proper relationship with each other. And by that time, I knew I was head over heels in love with him.

About six months later, we were lying in our lounge room watching TV when he turned to me suddenly and asked if his scars bothered me at all. I was a bit lost for words; I'd never really thought about it, I'd never known him any other way. I just looked at him and said truthfully: "No, they don't and never have." That was the only time he ever asked me about it.

The fact that he has serious burns scars has rarely been an issue for us. I've only ever seen a few times how much it affected him. One time in particular was a hot summer's day, and instead of putting on a T-shirt or singlet as he normally would, he chose a long-sleeve shirt. When I pointed out the obvious hot weather outside, he changed into a singlet but something didn't seem right.

We drove to the local shops and I noticed him looking around. I asked him what was wrong and he said: "Everyone's looking at me, everyone's staring at my scars!" I'd never seen him uncomfortable about it before and was completely thrown. Eventually we left and drove home in silence.

When we finally spoke about it, I told him I hadn't realised that he felt that way at times. He told me that he generally didn't any more but for some reason, he had that day. That was when I first realised how much it had affected him inside.

One of the challenges to being in a relationship with someone who's gone through a major personal trauma like Bali is that you tend to feel like an outsider, especially if your relationship started after the event. Phil seemed to be very aware of that, and so from very early on he made an effort to include me in that area of his life.

At first, I didn't know much about his story even though we lived together. But when the fifth anniversary came around in 2007, he decided to take part in a documentary.

Before it aired on television, he asked if I'd watch it with him. It was the first time that I was given details about what had happened to him, and we spoke at length about his experiences afterwards.

About six months later, Phil was approached to get involved in the Bali Peace Park project and he asked if I'd be a part of it with him. He told me he thought it would be a way to include me in that part of his life. He made it clear to me that I wasn't just a partner in his life "after Bali"; instead I was part of his life. Period. And that inevitably included both of us embracing his past.

I can't imagine what it was like for him to have gone through what he did. But one thing I do know is that he's the most amazing human being I've ever met. He inspires me and motivates me and has given me a love that I never thought possible, both the love for him as my husband and the beautiful gift of a mother's love for our children. The fact that he survived the Sari Club attacks in 2002 changed my life and my future forever, and for that I am eternally grateful.

25

A mother's view – looking back

FOR PHIL, IT WAS A SLOW AND GRADUAL RECOVERY. It's been a process, right up to now. When he went on the trip to Europe and the US I think that helped.

Reflecting back on it all, I'm just amazed at my son. He would have been a brilliant person regardless but now, in this way, he's going to be affecting so many more people's lives in such a positive way.

They say things happen for a reason, and for a long time we were all searching for the reason. In the end, I don't think that you can make sense of what those people did, but he's taken a really horrific thing and shone a light into it.

Out of respect for all the boys who lost their lives, he's spreading more humanity into everyone else. He's proving that war and terrorists and hatred are not worth anything; it's love and compassion that moves this world and he's proof of that.

I've always been really, really proud of him. I wish there were more people like him.

26

My message is simple –
appreciate, embrace and love

When I look back now, I can take a broader view of what I have been through. I've always had the view that life has a funny way of getting you where you're supposed to be and I often had to hold on to that belief to get me through the tough times. I was heading down one road and then things way out of my control took me in another direction.

I was left with some difficult issues to wrestle as I tried to figure out where my life was heading after 2002. But in a strange sort of way, if it had never happened, I probably wouldn't be where I am today. And where I am is an amazing place.

My life has moved on. I married the girl of my dreams, I'm a father, I'm a martial arts instructor and I have my own business.

I've thought about how often I wished I'd died, how many times I'd nearly given up, and I think now, if I had, I would have missed all this. It's just proved to me that even though you think you know what your future has in store for you, you actually have no idea.

The horror of what happened to me and so many other people can never be forgotten, and lots of people are still dealing with their issues. People were massacred just for being in the wrong place at the wrong time. They were murdered on the dance floor.

I've often wondered: if I hadn't been in the bombing, what sort of person would I be now? Would I be a better person? Would I be more of a ratbag?

When I think about it all or talk about it, the saying "When life gives you lemons, you make lemonade" often comes to mind. I was given some pretty rotten lemons but, somehow, I've managed to create something I'm proud of with my life. When I look back I realise I'm a much stronger person than I ever would have been, mentally and physically, if my life had not taken that twist.

I'm not saying that if I was given a choice, I would willingly go through what happened to me. But that's the point in life – a lot of the time, you don't choose, you just get dealt your hand. And that's why I think it's so important that when you are lucky enough to make decisions in life, you think them through carefully. Bad choices get you to the wrong place quicker than bad luck ever will.

I always come back to the idea that while life is full of challenges and adversity, it's only the strongest among us who are tested. Something that's been said to me along the way is: "You're one of the few who had the strength to get through it." It gives you a sense that others believe in your strength and your courage. I believe if you're being tested somehow, it's because you are able to overcome. You just need to figure out how.

What happened in Bali doesn't wholly define me, although it did for a while. Instead, it's a part of my past; it was a huge life-changing moment that altered me in many ways. It re-focused me and forced me to grow as a person.

The Bali bombings were a tragedy but surviving them was a gift, something I don't ever take for granted. And I hope that when I speak to people about what

I've been through, and that when I provide a positive example to martial arts classes, I have a life experience that will help others.

I'm honestly able to say well, look, life is tough sometimes, but that doesn't mean you can't get through it or change it. I tell people: "Don't wait for a tragedy before you make a change in your life. Do it now."

Don't live life with regrets. Appreciate what you have. Embrace life, chase your dreams and grab them with both hands, but also remember how precious life is, and that it can be taken away so quickly.

When I speak to younger people now I tell them: "Make sure you tell your mum and dad that you love them. You never know when it might be the last time you see them." And most of the time, it doesn't fall on deaf ears. I believe they hear me and do just that.

I hope I can help people realise they really do have the opportunity to change things, to live fuller, happier lives.

My message is simple — love life, love your family and friends, kiss your kids, and out of love, you'll find happiness.

IN MEMORIAM

AUSTRALIA (88)

Surname	Given Names
AIRLIE	Gayle
ALLEN	Belinda
ANDERSON	Renae Marie
BASIOLI	Peter Carlo
BETMALIK	Christina
BOLWERK	Mathew Lucas
BORGIA	Abbey
BORGIA	Deborah
BUCHAN (née BROUGHAM)	Gerardine Majella
BUCHAN	Stephen James (Fish)
BYRON	Chloé Blanche
CACHIA	Anthony Francis

CARTLEDGE	Rebecca Marie
CARTWRIGHT	Bronwyn Louise
CEARNS	Jodie Patricia
CORTEEN	Jane
CORTEEN	Jenny
CRONIN	Paul William
CROXFORD	Donna Loraine
CURNOW	Kristen
DAHAN	Francoise
DALAIS (née BALDACCHINO)	Sylvia
DEEGAN	Joshua (Josh)
DOBSON	Andrew Maurice
DUNLOP	Michelle (Shelley)
DUNN	Craig
FOLEY	Shane John
GALLAGHER	Dean Richard
GANE	Jared James
GOLOTTA	Angela Sylvia Rose
GRAY	Angela Simone
HANCOCK	Byron John
HANLEY	Simone Jane
HARDMAN	James Berkeley
HARDY	William (Billy) Roy
HARRISON	Nicole Maree
HAWKINS	Timothy Leigh (Jupes)
HORE	Andrea Michelle
HOWARD	Adam L

ILIFFE	Joshua Ives
JOHNSTONE	Carol
KENT	David Richard Charles
KOTRONAKIS	Dimitra (Dimmy)
KOTRONAKIS	Elizabeth (Lizzy)
LEE	Aaron James
LEE	Justin Graeme
LEE (née THORNBURGH)	Stacey Maree
LEWIS	Danny Robert John
LYSAGHT	Scott
MAKAWANA	Lynda
MALONEY	Suzanne
MARSHALL	Robert James (Bob)
MAVROUDIS	David
McKEON	Lynette Patricia
McKEON	Marissa Lee
MURPHY (née DEAKIN)	Jennifer Ann
O'DONNELL	Amber Sue
O'DONNELL	Jessica
OGIER (née FILIMAUA)	Susan Lona
O'SHEA	Jodie
PALTRIDGE	Corey
RIDLEY	Brad
ROBERTS	Ben
ROSS (née ROWLANDS)	Bronwyn (Bronch)
ROSS	David Cameron
SALVATORI (née HACKETT)	Kathy Ann

SANDERSON — Greg

SEELIN — Catherine Patricia

SEXTON — Lee Anthony

SINGER — Tom

STEVENSON — Julie

STEWART — Anthony Scott

STOKES — Jason Terrence

SÜMER — Behiç

SWAIN — Nathan Gregory

THOMAS — Tracy Ann

THOMPSON — Clint Nathan

THWAITES — Robert Rex

VANRENEN — Charles R D

WADE — Jonathon (Jono)

WALDER — Vanessa

WALLACE — Jodi Leigh

WALSH-TILL — Shane Patrick

WEBSTER — Robyn

WHITELEY — Marlene Taylor

WHITTON (née RINGK) — Charmaine Margaret

YEO — Gerard Michael

ZERVOS — Louiza

BRAZIL (2)

FARIAS — Marco Antonio

WATAKE — Alexandre Moraes

CANADA (2)

GLEASON — Richard

POPADYNEC — Mervin

DENMARK (3)

BØDKER — Laerke Cecilie

JENSEN — Annette Overgaard

KNUDSEN — Lise Tanghus

ECUADOR (1)

AVILES — Ana Cecilia

FRANCE (4)

BREANT — Guillaume

ERISEY — Lionel

MORDELET — Manuel

UNDERWOOD — Anthony

GERMANY (6)

BRANDES — Bettina Christina

HAUKE — Udo Paul

KOHNKE — Angelika Helene

KÖPPKE — Alexandra

THEILE — Claudia Dietlinde

WENDT — Marie-Cécile

GREECE (1)

PANAGOULAS — Dimitris N

INDONESIA (38)

ARISMUNANDAR	
ARMANSYAH	Rudy
ARTINI	Gusti Ayn Made
BADRAWAN	I Gede
CANDRA	I Komang
CINDRA	I Ketut
DUKA	Tata
ENDANG	
FATURRAHMAN	
HANNY	
JUNIARDI	
KHOTIB	Mochamad
MARGARINI	Ni Kadek Alit
MAWA	I Nyoman
MERTANA	Made
MUGIANTO	
NGARTINA	I Kadek
PRIMA	I Kadek Beni
PUSPITA	Lilis
RAHMAT	Arsoyo
SARDJONO	Imawan
SAVITRII	Ati
SIMANJUNTAK	Jonathan
SINGH	Salwindar
SUHARTO	Elly Susanti
SUHARTO	Achmad

SUHERI	Agus
SUJANA	I Made
SUKADANA	I Wayan
SUKERNA	Kadek
SUMERAWAT	I Ketut
TAMBA	I Wayan
WIBOWO	R Destria Bimo Adhi
WIDAYATI	
WIJA	I Made
WIJAYA	I Made
WIJAYA	I Ketut Nana
YUSTARA	I Wayan

ITALY (1)

| SBIRONI | Roberto Antonio |

JAPAN (2)

| SUZUKI | Kosuke |
| SUZUKI | Yuka |

NETHERLANDS (4)

FRERIKS	Norbert Edgar
HARSKAMP	Sander
SCHIPPERS	Mark Antonio
VAN LIJNEN NOOMEN	Marjanne

NEW ZEALAND (2)

PARKER	Mark
WELLINGTON	Jamie

POLAND (1)

PAWLAK	Danuta Beata

PORTUGAL (1)

DANTAS RIBEIRINHO	Diogo Miguel

SOUTH AFRICA (2)

FITZ	Godfrey
HARTY	Craig Russell

SOUTH KOREA (2)

MOON	Eun Jung
MOON	Eun Young

SWEDEN (5)

BERGANDER	Johanna
CRONQVIST	Linda
GUSTAFSSON	Ulrika
JOHANSSON	Maria
RÄFLING	Carina

SWITZERLAND (3)

DOLF — Pascal Michael
LIESCH — Sereina
RUPP — Gian Andrea

TAIWAN (1)

HUI-MIN — Kuo

UNITED KINGDOM (23)

ARNOLD — Timothy
BOWLER — Neil
BRADEN — Daniel
BRADFORD — Christopher
ELLWOOD — Jonathon
EMPSON — Lucy S. O.
FINDLEY — Ian
FOX — Emma Louise
FRANCE — Laura
GAJARDO — Mark
HOLMES — Tom
HUSSEY — Paul Martin
KAYS — Christopher John
LINDÉN — Annika Kerstin
MILLER — Nathaniel (Dan)
PERKINS — Natalie
RECORD — Peter
REDMAN — Christian

SPEIRS	Stevie
STANDRING	Michael
WALLER	Ed
WALTON	Clive John
WARNER	Douglas

UNITED STATES (7)

CASNER	Karri Jane
HEFFERNAN	Megan Eileen
MCCORMICK II	Robert Alan
MILLIGAN	George Hamilton
SNODGRASS	Deborah Lea
WEBSTER	Steven Brooks
YOUNG	Jacob Cardwell

UNIDENTIFIED (3)

Unidentified 1
Unidentified 2
Unidentified 3

TOTAL – 202

[Source: Bali Memorial, Kuta and Australian Consulate General, Bali]